MEDIA

THE

PEAK PRACTICE

COMPANION

THE
PEAK
PRACTICE
COMPANION

Deborah & Anthony Hayward

ORION

CARLTON

CONTENTS

Many people have helped us in our research for this book. We would particularly like to thank the following: creator Lucy Gannon; producers Tony Virgo, Michele Buck and Damien Timmer; producer's assistant Karol-Ann Pearson; associate producer Helga Dowie; production designer Jeff Tessler; composer John Altman; chief production buyer John Steppings; medical advisers Dr Tim Parkin and Helen Holmes; stunt co-ordinators Roy Alon and Alan Stuart; stunt performer Abbi Collins; second assistant director Radford Neville; cast members Gary Mavers, Saskia Wickham, Adrian Lukis, Fiona Gillies, Clive Swift, Esther Coles, Richard Platt, Hazel Ellerby, Margery Mason, Geoffrey Bayldon and Judy Brooke; programme publicist Fiona Johnston; Geoff Mayor and the picture library at Carlton's Nottingham studios; Patrick Smith at the Carlton picture library in London; Siân Facer and Dawn Steele at Carlton Licensing; and Trevor Dolby at Orion Media. We would also like to thank Brian and Marlene Jones, and Danielle, Clare, Alexander and Olivia.

First published in 1998 by Orion Media
An imprint of Orion Books Ltd
Orion House
5 Upper St Martin's Lane
London WC2H 9EA

A CIP catalogue record for this book is available from the British Library.

ISBN 0-75281-788-4

Printed in Italy by Printers, Trento

Bound by L.E.G.O., Vicenza

FOREWORD

*S*oldier Soldier had been a massive hit for screenwriter Lucy Gannon, *Boon* had ended and Central Television was looking for another popular drama that would capture the imaginations of viewers. At the same time, Kevin Whately was ending his run as Sergeant Lewis in *Inspector Morse* and looking for a new television role.

Switching from using her experience as a military policewoman, which helped her to create *Soldier Soldier*, to the years she spent in nursing, Lucy longed to write a medical drama set around three GPs in a rural practice. When she put the characters and story in the setting of her home county, Derbyshire, a television phenomenon was created.

After six series, *Peak Practice* is one of the most successful television series ever and, after a complete change of cast, has proved to be one of those rare programmes where the production is bigger than the stars. We hope that this book whips up a flavour of all those ingredients – characters, story and setting – that have made *Peak Practice* one of television's best-loved programmes.

Deborah & Anthony Hayward

OUT OF AFRICA
– AND LUCY'S PEN

THE CREATOR

Lucy Gannon did not turn to writing until the age of 39, when she won the 1986 Richard Burton Award for her play *Keeping Tom Nice*, about a handicapped boy and the strain caring for him put on his family. It was her first piece of writing since school.

Born in Londonderry, Lucy was the daughter of a soldier. She was only seven when she experienced the trauma of her mother dying, and her childhood was spent, accompanying her father on postings around the world, from Colchester to Cyprus. After school, Lucy worked as a military policewoman for 18 months before switching to a career in nursing.

Dr Jack Kerruish roared out of Africa in his jeep and headed for home after three years working in a remote Zimbabwean village at the Dry River Clinic, which he helped to set up from scratch. On his return to England, the idealistic but flawed doctor finally ditched the girlfriend he had left behind in London and dreamed of seeking a fresh challenge as a country GP.

An advert for a doctor to join a surgery in the picturesque Peak District appeared to offer Jack the opportunity he craved: to become indispensable to the residents of a small community. But Dr Beth Glover, who had inherited The Beeches practice from her father, was not impressed. She thought his long hair would not endear him to her conservative patients in the Derbyshire village of Cardale, and sent him away deflated.

However, on deciding that she had been hasty, Beth reconsidered and invited Jack to join her and junior partner Dr Will Preston in the practice. Jack's drive and ambition were just the qualities The Beeches needed in order to compete with the new health centre that had opened in the

RIGHT *Jack Kerruish (Kevin Whately) left the Dry River Clinic in Zimbabwe to join Beth Glover (Amanda Burton) in her rural Derbyshire practice in Lucy Gannon's new series of medical dramas.*

When Lucy's engineer husband, George, lost his job, she became the sole breadwinner. Thanks to her job as a care assistant in a hostel for the mentally handicapped, she was able to support George and her daughter, Louise, in the family's house on a Derby council estate.

Purely in the hope of winning £2,000 to buy a car, she entered the Richard Burton Award for aspiring playwrights. She happily accepted the money when *Keeping Tom Nice*, which was drawn from her own experience working in the health service, won, but she turned down the other part of the prize – a six-month spell as writer-in-residence at the Royal Shakespeare Company – because she could not afford to give up her job. When Richard Burton's widow, Sally, found out, she phoned Lucy and offered her six months' salary, enabling her to take up the residency.

Keeping Tom Nice was performed on the London stage and when, in 1989, it was adapted for television, with John Alderton and Gwen Taylor starring, Lucy decided to become a full-time writer.

Lucy's big television break came when Central Television asked her to write a television series about army wives. Insisting that she wanted to write about women and men, Lucy came up with *Soldier Soldier* and folk heroes Paddy Garvey and Dave Tucker. Holly Aird's character, Nancy, was based on her own short-lived experiences in the Army. The programme, whose long run began in 1991, was an immediate success.

Lucy followed it with *Peak Practice* and has since created and written another successful ITV series, *Bramwell*, about a female doctor running a hospital in London's East End in the Victorian era. She also wrote the 'Screen One' dramas *Tender Loving Care*, featuring Dawn French as a homicidal nurse, and *Trip Trap*, starring former *Peak Practice* star Kevin Whately as a wife batterer, as well as the BBC prison series *Insiders*. Lucy was made an MBE in the 1997 New Year's honours list.

village. A glint in Beth's eye signalled that Jack's allure was down to more than his medical capabilities. Could it be that theirs was destined to be more than a working partnership?

Peak Practice was Britain's most successful new drama of 1993 and attracted more than 14 million viewers by the end of the second series, becoming a programme that would return to ITV screens year after year.

TED MAKES THE DIAGNOSIS

Peak Practice was conceived out of the desire by the managing director of Central Films, Ted Childs, to find a new role for actor Kevin Whately after his long run as John Thaw's sidekick, Sgt Lewis, in *Inspector Morse*. He also needed a programme to take the place of *Boon*, which had just finished production at Central's Nottingham studios.

Ted, a veteran producer of series such as *Special Branch* and *The Sweeney* before becoming Central Television's controller of drama, decided to approach Derby-based writer Lucy Gannon. She had already given the company a huge success by creating the ITV series *Soldier Soldier*, which had found such a wide audience by telling the fictional stories of soldiers and their wives. He also appointed a producer, Tony Virgo, who had previously worked on *EastEnders* and *The Bill*.

'Ted Childs told me that the new programme was to come out of the Nottingham studios, so it had to be Midlands-based,' says Lucy. 'They wanted a long-running series like *Soldier Soldier*, but didn't mind what it was. I knew it had to be something where every week there

Sending Jack on a cave rescue enabled creator Lucy Gannon and producer Tony Virgo to show the beauty of the Peak District.

would be a complete story – beginning, middle and end – with a gradually developing strand all the way through for the main characters.

'I knew that Kevin Whately wanted to do a series for Central, but there were several others who wanted to as well. So we had quite a range of people available. I really value Kevin's acting, which I think is topnotch. Given the group I had to consider, Kevin kept coming to the fore for me, although he might have decided that he didn't like the scripts. The programme would have gone ahead anyway, so I knew the lead role had to be something that wasn't so tightly tailored that it would put off any other actor.

'We went down the usual route of looking at all the professions, such as the law and police, but I hankered after doing something about doctors, because at that time there was nothing on television apart from *Casualty*, which was a very particular type of medical drama. In those days,

Casualty was purely trauma. With a medical series, the possibilities are absolutely endless and the appeal is universal – we're all ill at some time, we all know people who are ill and we all have doctors.

'Central had suggested that we use the Belvoir Valley, near Nottingham, as the setting for the GPs' practice. So I met the producer, Tony Virgo, in Nottingham one day and we went out in my car and looked at that area and both felt that it wasn't the place we wanted to set a drama. We thought it was quite "safely" rural, a bit manicured really and not dramatic enough. Also, because it was so near a large city, there would have been fewer story possibilities.

'So we went to the Peaks, which I knew quite well through living near Derby. We looked all round Crich, Holloway and the other places in which we eventually set it, and just fell in love with the area. I started looking at the population there, the levels of employment, where they worked, the ages of the people and the size of the practice.

'There were to be three doctors and in the second series they would be going into fundholding, which was a political issue. When we started the programme, not many doctors were going into it, so we made a positive virtue of that before we eventually went into it.'

LUCY PRESENTS THE PRESCRIPTION

With the concept and setting established, Ted Childs asked Lucy to prepare a 'Bible' for the new series, outlining details of The Beeches surgery, the three doctors, receptionist, the practice nurse, and a demography of the area. She also originated ten sto-

rylines and wrote two of the scripts. These were well-received and resulted in *Peak Practice* being commissioned as an eight-part series due to be screened on ITV during the spring of 1993.

In deciding the mix of characters, Lucy kept to the principles that had made *Soldier Soldier* such a success. 'I would hate to write a series that is mainly about men or about women,' she explains. 'I think that all the fun and drama in life comes from men and women together, so I knew there would have to be a mix of both in the surgery.

'I wanted two men in the programme and, being quite practical about it, there are a lot of receptionists and practice nurses in GPs' surgeries and not many are men, so we had two male doctors and one female one.

'We came up with three very different characters: Will Preston, an ex-public schoolboy who was in an unhappy marriage and had great aspirations to make money, and would in the second series have a nervous breakdown, partly because of the pressures he placed upon himself; Jack Kerruish, an idealistically dedicated man who could be quite stupidly dedicated and idealistic sometimes; and Beth Glover, a woman who was battling between these two as the senior partner.'

In writing the 'Bible', Lucy decided that each week there would be no more than two strong emotional stories so that each could be given 'good weight' and explored, with one of the doctors predominating in each episode. Her other stipulations were that there would be plenty of humour, no sentimentality and no political bias.

Lucy, Ted Childs and Tony Virgo then met Kevin Whately to find out his reaction to the concept for *Peak Practice*. 'He quite liked the "Bible" and said he would proba-

Beth proposes to Jack after he rescues her in an outlying area of the
Peak District following her attempt to save the victim of a car crash.

bly do the programme, but he wanted to see the scripts before committing himself,' recalls Lucy. 'Then I started writing them and Kevin came to lunch with me and my husband, George, and agreed to do the programme. Shortly afterwards, George died very suddenly of a heart attack, which threw everything into a spin. As a result, I can't remember much of the first series. I just sat at home and wrote.'

'Kevin was in a position where he didn't want to step into something that wasn't very good,' says Tony Virgo. 'He wanted to see what it was like. Kevin put a lot of effort into the role and talked a lot about it.

It's very easy for us to put a lot of "back story" into the character, about him coming back from Africa, but it doesn't mean anything. How you cut through it is really what it's about and whether viewers like the character. Some actors don't do enough work at that stage, but Kevin really did. We just talked about it so much – what Jack was, where he was going and what type of programme we were going to do.

'I was very keen to do something along the lines of the American series *thirtysomething*, which I loved at that time. What I thought was brilliant about it was its in-depth themes about human emotions. I

THE BEECHES

The Beeches, which Dr Beth Glover originally inherited on her father's death, is a three-partner practice. It has more than 7,000 patients registered with it, and holds surgeries between 8.30 and 11.30am and 4.00 and 6.00pm. The doctors undertake home visits in the intervening hours and also run antenatal and other clinics.

The surgery has a reception area, three consulting rooms and a treatment room where minor operations are peformed. Patient records are kept in a computer system introduced by Jack Kerruish on his arrival in Cardale.

Shared night cover with the Brompton Health Centre finished in 1997 when the centre pulled out of the scheme, but Dr Erica Matthews came up with the idea of forming a co-op with other practices. However, Dr David Shearer and practice nurse Laura Elliott feared that this would result in patients being treated by doctors who did not know their medical history. Their deep reservations were confirmed when a young leukaemia sufferer's condition was not recognised by another doctor – with tragic consequences – and, as a result, Erica pulled out of the co-op.

The nearest hospital is almost half-an-hour away, so GPs at The Beeches have to be competent paramedics, able to deal with emergencies in a rural area.

They made additional money through the surgery's dispensary, but they were forced to close it when Norman Shorthose opened a chemist shop in Cardale in 1998.

When The Beeches was first seen in 1993, it faced competition from the Brompton Health Centre, which was set up by Dr John Reginald to service the needs of residents on a new housing estate. Since the curtailment of that development, the health centre has not expanded as much as expected, although it does take private patients.

A year later, The Beeches became a fundholding practice, managing its own budgets for drugs, patient services, staff – excluding doctors – and overall management for items such as office equipment. Fundholding will cease to exist in April 1999.

hoped that *Peak Practice* could do that in a British series that wasn't really about doctoring but emotional contact between human beings, and Lucy gave us the platform to do that.'

Tony was so enthusiastic about the new programme that he rejected another job even before *Peak Practice* was commissioned by ITV. 'I had just been offered *Taggart*, which was something I loved and always wanted to do, and was about to sign for it,' says Tony. 'No one was sure whether *Peak Practice* would be commissioned, but I turned down *Taggart* and waited for *Peak Practice* to get the go-ahead because I felt all the ingredients of the series seemed just right.'

CASTING

With the green light to go into production, and Kevin Whately having agreed to take the role of Jack, auditions were held to cast the other parts, most importantly those of Beth Glover and Will Preston. Casting sessions were overseen by Tony, casting director Julia Lisney, and Gordon Flemyng, one of four directors assigned to the first series.

Barbara Flynn and Zoë Wanamaker both turned down the role of Beth. Eventually, a shortlist of five actresses was auditioned, including Amanda Burton. She was recommended by Gordon Flemyng, who had worked with the former *Brookside* star on an episode of *Minder*, in which she played a solicitor prosecuting Arthur Daley. Amanda had also starred alongside Michael Elphick in one series of *Boon*, which was also made by Central Television.

'We all agreed on Amanda,' says Tony. 'Although she had done *Brookside*, she wasn't really a star. Gordon was batting very heavily for her at the beginning and, when we saw her, she was just charming. She had a lightness of touch, was fun and absolutely sexy. I just felt the hairs go up on my back when I saw her and talked to her.

'Gordon and I went up to Ted Childs and said we'd like to go for Amanda Burton and he asked what she had done. He asked us: "Are you sure about this?" We told him we were sure, and he replied: "Well, I hope you're right." And that was that.'

Simon Shepherd was cast as the third doctor, Will Preston, following his role as Piers Garfield-Ward in the Central series *Chancer*. The part of Beth's good friend Isabel de Gines went to Sylvia Syms, a leading lady of the British cinema in the fifties and sixties.

'I liked Simon in *Chancer*, although, again, he wasn't a star,' recalls Tony. 'We wanted three different views in this practice. For Will, we wanted a doctor with a public-school background, who wasn't trying enough but there was something in him that could rise to the challenge.

'Simon was good-looking and tried so hard, but at first he had reservations about taking the role. Kevin and Amanda had already been cast and he wondered if there was enough in it for him, but we convinced Simon that all the doctors would have their own running stories.

'We floated actresses' names around for the role of Isabel, and Julian Murphy, the script editor, suggested Sylvia Syms. Having worked with her years earlier in the *Nancy*

Astor series, I thought she was brilliant, although I have to admit that she scared the pants off me. But, underneath all that, she is the nicest person. I fought for Sylvia to get the role.'

The combination of Ted Childs's search for a new series and Lucy Gannon and Tony Virgo's desire to write about a doctors' practice in the beautiful Peak District had resulted in the creation of a programme that would appeal to viewers across the nation. It was also about to put the Derbyshire countryside on the television map.

Lucy Gannon created Peak Practice *when Central Television was looking for another long-running series like her previous series,* Soldier Soldier. *Once the concept of a drama set in a GPs' practice in the Peaks was decided, Lucy started to write.*

PICK OF THE PEAKS

The Derbyshire village of Crich, south of Matlock, was chosen as the setting for the fictional Cardale in *Peak Practice*. It was the nearest village to Central Television's Nottingham studios that had an authentic Peak District look, and provided a community large enough to make a three-doctor practice plausible.

The Peak District National Park has been in existence since 1951 to protect this area of England, and stretches from the countryside north of Derby to within a short distance of the small West Yorkshire town of Holmfirth, made famous most recently by the television series *Last of the Summer Wine*.

The Peaks, boasting 542 square miles of moors and dales, ravines and crags, beautiful flora and fauna, and a population of only 40,000, became the first of 11 national parks intended as places to which those in the industrial areas of England could get away from it all in the post-war years.

CRICH

Before *Peak Practice* arrived, Crich was best known as the home of the National Tramway Museum, which houses steam-driven, horse-driven and electric trams from all over Britain and the world. The village has been used for filming shops in the series such as the Cardale Fish and Chip Shop and Allsop's Bakery, as well as Beth Glover's home. The small village greengrocer's shop was converted into the local bank, seen in the first series of *Peak Practice*, and Isabel de Gines's home was a big, double-fronted, early-Victorian house in Crich that needed very little changed when filming began.

'What I like about Crich,' says Jeff Tessler, production designer on *Peak Practice* since the beginning of the second series, 'is that it has shops and some scale to it, and it's not a "chocolate box" country village. It has a bit more of a rough edge to

The filming of scenes in Cardale takes place in the real life village of Crich, chosen as the right size for a three-partner GPs' practice.

The beautiful Peak District has provided a picturesque and dramatic backdrop to Peak Practice.

it, so stories don't inevitably have to be rural in the way that they would be in *All Creatures Great and Small* in the Yorkshire Dales.

'The Baptist church, which has a strong façade, has a very Northern look. Also, Crich has hills around it and within it, and it's really just a meeting point of five roads, which means it's difficult to film in because of traffic, but it does give that edge to the programme.'

Jeff acknowledges that *Peak Practice* gives a romantic view of the countryside in and around Crich. 'It's not what it's really like,' he says. 'For instance, as you drive around the area you see that it's blighted by quar-

ries and the lorries that go to and from them. Every alternate house will have been built since the sixties.

'Most people in the countryside don't live in idyllic stone cottages, but that's what we've created in Cardale. A lot of people actually live in brick houses with central heating, but we go for nice stone cottages with smoke coming out of chimneys.'

THE BEECHES

A location for The Beeches surgery was found half a mile away from Crich at a property called Chestnut Bank in Fritchley,

Chestnut Bank, Fritchley, was chosen as the house to convert into a doctors' surgery – and The Beeches was born.

an 18th-century farmhouse that had once been a Quaker school and, more recently, converted into three flats. 'It's very hard to find somewhere to use as a doctor's surgery,' says Jeff. 'You can't use a real doctor's surgery, for obvious reasons, and very few empty houses are big enough to use.

'After trawling around estate agents, a house was found in Fritchley that was large enough to convert, with quite big rooms, enough parking space for the production team's vehicles and equipment, as well as the fictional doctors' cars, nice views out of the windows and no passing traffic to worry about while filming.'

For the second series, The Beeches was redecorated and its layout changed slightly to give more room for filming the doctors in their rooms. 'You learn from experience what is useful,' says Jeff. 'We changed a lot of the colours and used some rooms more than others.'

THE MANOR HOTEL

The Manor Hotel in South Wingfield, a few miles north of Crich, provides the interiors of the pub of the same name in the story, run by James and Chloë White. 'The owners are happy to close while we're filming because it's relatively quiet during the day,' says Jeff.

Nearby Wingfield Manor, in the same village, has been used as a filming location several times during the programme's history, such as when an epileptic boy became trapped on the ledge of a derelict building in 1994 and as the setting for a village pageant three years later.

The property, now mostly in ruins and owned by English Heritage, was once one of Mary, Queen of Scots's main prisons. It

has also been seen in the children's television series *The Chronicles of Narnia* and in Franco Zeffirelli's film version of *Jane Eyre*.

DOCTORS' HOUSES

Jack Kerruish stayed at The Manor Hotel during the first series of *Peak Practice*, but

then bought a house in Cardale, which Central Television actually filmed at Melkridge House, a holiday cottage in Fritchley. Beth's cottage was, in reality, Archway House, next to the Black Swan pub in Crich. 'Beth's house was very small and difficult to film inside,' says Jeff Tessler, 'but it was chosen because it was in the middle of Crich and established her as part of the community – it was very much *her* village.'

When Jack and Beth married, they needed more room.

Archway House, next to the Black Swan pub in Crich, became Beth's home.

Although their new home was supposed to be in Cardale, it was really in Starkholmes. 'It was an absolutely stunning ex-coaching house,' says Jeff. 'We redecorated and refurnished it and the family lived with our furniture for almost a year. Because the focal point of the third series was Jack and Beth's relationship, we spent a lot of time in that house and a lot of money on getting it looking right.'

Will Preston's original home, with his wife and children, was also filmed in Crich, although the film crew had to contend with noise from a nearby road. For the second series, as the Prestons traded down in an attempt to live within their means, filming moved to a smaller, less attractive, late-Victorian, semi-detached town house in Matlock, although it remained in Cardale in the story. Later, a divorced Will was living in a flat, so his front door was filmed in the market square in Crich, but an interior was set up in a storeroom on the top floor of the building used as The Beeches, in Fritchley.

When, at the start of the fourth series, Will moved into a new house just outside Cardale, it was actually an attractive, double-fronted Georgian house filmed 22 miles west of Crich, in the centre of the picturesque village of Hartington. At the same time, Andrew Attwood moved into Will's old flat.

For the next series, Andrew rented a small cottage with very few items of furniture, which in reality was in Holloway, between Crich and Matlock. 'In the story, he still had his house in Liverpool but was separated from his wife, Kirsty,' says Jeff, 'so he rented somewhere and never did much to it. Then he spent all his money buying a house but had nothing to spend on it until Erica Matthews moved in and started to brighten the place up with pictures on the walls and cushions. We found that cottage in Wheatcroft, between Crich and Matlock.'

Erica's first house, a semi-derelict cottage that she then refurbished, burned down in the 1997 series. Jeff discovered a suitable property in the village of Idridgehay, east of the market town of Ashbourne, for the dramatic storyline. 'It wasn't actually derelict,' he explains. 'It was a very nice little cottage, normally rented out. We pulled out the carpets and curtains, dirtied down the walls and aged it. During that series, in 1997, we gradually put everything back – until we set fire to it. We built a block on the end of the cottage with a three-storey stone chimney breast so we could set it alight. Erica then lived upstairs at The Manor Hotel until Andrew persuaded her to move in with him.'

David and Clare Shearer bought their remote, old farmhouse at the beginning of the fifth series and gradually set about turning it into a home. Jeff added more furniture and pictures, and added some wall tiling. The real-life house, near the village of Wessington, between Crich and Matlock, belongs to *Peak Practice*'s medical adviser, Dr Tim Parkin. 'It's one of those houses that you see and immediately know it will work,' says Jeff.

OTHER LOCATIONS

Panoramic shots of the beautiful countryside around Crich have usually been filmed in Holloway – the childhood home of Florence Nightingale – and around Matlock. Caverns at the Heights of Abraham, based in the town, were used as the setting for Jack's dramatic cave rescue at the start of the second series.

Jack and Beth's wedding in the same

series took place at Holy Trinity Church in the village of Kirk Ireton, south of Matlock, with a carriage supplied by The Red House Stables and Carriage Museum at Darley Dale, north of Matlock on the A6 towards Bakewell. Other churches seen in the programme have included one in Starkholmes, next to the location used for Jack and Beth's house, and one on the Chatsworth estate for the 'non wedding' of Erica and Andrew.

Various hospitals have been used for filming since *Peak Practice* started, including the Queen's Medical Centre in Nottingham, Derby City General Hospital, King's Mill Hospital in Mansfield and Derby Royal Infirmary.

Norman Shorthose's Cardale pharmacy, introduced in 1998, was in reality a former post office in the middle of Bonsall, near Matlock Bath, and a chemist was brought in to 'dress' the interior to look authentic. Paul Biant, who had previously advised *Peak Practice* on the appearance of prescription drugs and their effects, based it on his own shop in Nottingham.

Filming each series of *Peak Practice* normally takes eight months. Since the second series, the programme's production office has been based in the market town of Belper, famous for nail-making in the industrial revolution. The office is located on the site of the first mill built by patriarchal Jedediah Strutt, a former partner of Sir Richard Arkwright, who revolutionised the cotton industry with his invention of the spinning frame in 1769.

Norman Shorthose's pharmacy in Crich was, in reality, filmed in Bonsall, near Matlock Bath.

1993

Television's newest doctors made their début in a 90-minute opening episode of *Peak Practice* at 8.30pm on Monday, 10 May 1993, before switching to a regular hour-long slot starting at 9pm. The first episode saw Dr Jack Kerruish leave the clinic he had set up for a small community in Zimbabwe, finish with girlfriend Sandy after just two weeks back in London, and head for the Peak District village of Cardale to join Beth Glover and Will Preston in their rural practice. In Beth, the dashing, idealistic Jack met his match – both were obstinate and had an impulsive streak, guaranteeing that sparks would fly between them.

Beth, the senior partner, had taken over The Beeches after her father's death and faced competition from the Brompton Health Centre being set up in the village by the ruthless Dr John Reginald, who had already poached her other partner, the ambitious Dr Daniel Acres. The new GPs would be fundholders – something Beth had resisted so far but would eventually come to accept. This was the early nineties and fundholding was a harsh economic reality.

The eight episodes, costing almost £4 million in total, were an instant hit. The characters and stories, set against the backdrop of Derbyshire's Peak District, attracted more than 13 million viewers – making it the most successful new television drama series of 1993. While the BBC had major disappointments during the year with *A Year in Provence*, *The Riff Raff Element* and *Westbeach*, in *Peak Practice*, ITV had another drama to add to its string of continuing hits such as *Soldier Soldier* and *Heartbeat*.

Creator Lucy Gannon wrote most of the episodes, but others were devised by her and then written by Andy de la Tour, brother of actress Frances, or Tony Etchells, who had previously worked on *EastEnders* and *The Bill*.

Although Jack Kerruish saw himself as some kind of Superman, coming to the rescue of all in need, newspaper critics applauded the fact that he and his fellow doctors – including Will, whose crumbling marriage would eventually lead to a nervous breakdown – were less than perfect. 'Unlike *Casualty*, *Medics* and every other drama series about the medical profession since *Dr Finlay's Casebook*,' wrote Jill Parsons in the *Daily Mail*, '*Peak Practice* almost seems to invite the viewer to question the human fallibility of its central characters.'

Simon Shepherd, Kevin Whately and Amanda Burton and starred in Peak Practice *and were soon attracting more than 13 million viewers each week.*

THE CHARACTERS

DR JACK KERRUISH (Kevin Whately)
After a failed marriage and a half-hearted relationship with girlfriend Sandy, charismatic Jack returns to Britain after spending three years setting up a clinic in Africa and seeks life as a rural GP. He had previously spent ten years working in an inner-city area.

DR BETH GLOVER (Amanda Burton)
Senior partner at The Beeches, which she inherited from her father, Beth is a good doctor but a hopeless businesswoman. Fiercely independent, she is stubborn and headstrong – qualities she shares with Jack.

DR WILL PRESTON (Simon Shepherd)
The junior partner, Will is a public-school cynic who prefers a round of golf to putting effort into his job. With two sons, Tony and Julian, who attend public school, Will and wife Sarah live beyond their means and face a crisis in their marriage.

ISABEL DE GINES (Sylvia Syms)
Local magistrate and lifelong friend and confidante of Beth Glover, Isabel is the only person who will stand up to Beth – until Jack's arrival. She has lived in Cardale all her life and is well-respected.

SARAH PRESTON (Jacqueline Leonard)
Materialistic and anxious to shake off her working-class background, Will's wife, Sarah, berates her husband for not being assertive enough. Her desire to live a luxury life style causes financial problems, adding additional strain to their already shaky marriage.

KIM BEARDSMORE (Esther Coles)
Loyal receptionist at The Beeches, Kim – a single mother with a four-year-old son, Sam – is scatty and slightly disorganised but popular with patients, who find her warm and friendly.

ELLIE NDEBALA (Sharon Hinds)
Practice nurse at The Beeches, Ellie was brought up by a white couple after being given up for adoption by her natural parents, who were from Ghana. Single-minded and sensitive to criticism, Ellie turned down an offer to join the new health centre in Cardale after four years at The Beeches.

DR JOHN REGINALD (Andrew Ray)
Ruthless and willing to see The Beeches go under, Reginald is senior partner at the new Brompton Health Centre, which he has set up largely with his own money. He also runs a private clinic.

DR DANIEL ACRES (Tom Beard)
Poached by John Reginald to join the new health centre, Daniel was the third partner at The Beeches, but he was persuaded to move by an offer of a bigger salary.

JAMES and CHLOE WHITE
(Richard Platt and Hazel Ellerby)
Landlord and landlady of Cardale's popular pub, The Manor Hotel, James and Chloë – patients of Beth – are desperate to have children after years of trying without success.

ALICE NORTH (Margery Mason)
A cantankerous pensioner whom the doctors try to avoid, Alice – whose husband, Bob, died from stomach cancer – is often seen in the company of war veteran Douglas Hart.

TREVOR SHARP (Shaun Prendergast)
Cardale's part-time bank manager, Trevor is under pressure from Dr Reginald and Dr Acres to freeze The Beeches' overdraft.

LEANDA (Beth Goddard)
A local hairdresser, Leanda is passionately in love with bank manager Trevor Sharp and is willing to act out his sexual fantasies.

JACK AND THE BEECHES

In deepest Africa, Dr Jack Kerruish bade farewell to the friends and colleagues he had known for the last three years whilst building up the Dry River Clinic in an out-of-the-way part of Zimbabwe. His mission complete, he returned to England and long-term girlfriend Sandy, who lived in a trendy singles flat in London and worked for a publishing company, and started looking for a new job.

Determined to become a GP somewhere far away from the hustle and bustle of city life, Jack applied for a post at The Beeches, a small country practice in the Derbyshire Peak District. Inherited by Dr Beth Glover from her father, The Beeches' existence was threatened by the arrival of a smart new health centre in the village run by the

HOME AND ABROAD

Filming of *Peak Practice*'s opening scenes was done in Harare, the capital of Zimbabwe, showing Jack Kerruish during his final days at the Dry River Clinic. It took three days, giving give Jack a credible background story before returning to Britain.

'Our production manager said to me that he used to work for ITC on programmes such as *The Saint* and they filmed their African scenes on a backlot at Pinewood Studios,' recalls producer Tony Virgo. 'But we filmed ten minutes' footage for less than £40,000. It was a bit surreal going out there, then returning to Britain to film the rest of the series.

'As we made the programme, I really thought we had something because everyone cared so much about it. We planned quite well what was going to happen to the characters and were quite ruthless about the scripts. We were a bit thrown when there was one script that we had to ditch because it was so lame, not having the emotional depth of the others. This meant we had to bring other scripts forward and change the arc of the story slightly.'

IN TUNE WITH VIEWERS

Top film and TV composer John Altman came up with the distinctive, award-winning theme for *Peak Practice* and has continued to write and arrange all original music used in the programme.

'I was initially contacted by Tony Virgo, the producer, who had heard my score for the film *Hear My Song*,' recalls John, who also wrote the ship's orchestra music for the Oscar-winning picture *Titanic*. 'He liked certain elements of it and thought I might be sympathetic to the idea of his series.

'We wanted to get away from the fairly traditional music you find in medical programmes and to combine a British-countryside feeling with an African element, because Jack Kerruish was returning from Zimbabwe. He also liked Eric Clapton's guitar music, so we combined all those elements into one theme. It starts off fairly pastoral, followed by a break with the African thumb piano, then the two guitars crash in before all the themes join together. Many people didn't realise there was an African thumb piano – they thought the sound was supposed to represent the bleeping of an electronic machine in a hospital!'

• Jack Kerruish's first port of call on returning home from Zimbabwe was his girlfriend, Sandy, played by **Melanie Thaw**, who was no stranger to Kevin Whately. The actress is the stepdaughter of John Thaw, whom Kevin had starred alongside in *Inspector Morse*, and she had played Sue Lawrence in the second series of *Trainer*.

In *Peak Practice*, Sandy was the yuppie girl-friend whom Jack had left behind when he went to Africa. On his return, he tried life in her Docklands flat in London, but knew that he wanted to seek a challenge far away from the capital. She did not, and their relationship ended.

Melanie, whose mother, actress Sheila Hancock, encouraged her to study science rather than enter acting, recalls, 'It was strange to be working with someone who already knew everything about me through my father. Nowadays, I just take it for granted that so many people I work with are bound to have worked with my parents at some stage or other.

'I think my mum was quite keen on my being a doctor or a physicist. But, if I'm honest, I would have to say I never really thought enthusiastically about any profession other than acting.'

unscrupulous Dr John Reginald, who had already lured Dr Daniel Acres away from her and hoped to get all her patients as well. He plotted to close down The Beeches by persuading local bank manager Trevor Sharp to freeze its overdraft.

At his interview, Jack lay his past before Beth and practice junior partner Dr Will Preston. He told them of Africa, a broken marriage and his current failing relationship. Despite his frankness, Jack was turned down by Beth, who thought that his long hair made him too unconventional for staid, rural Cardale. She felt that he would only alienate people, and she could not see him doing 'internals on elderly virgins'.

Believing that she might have been hasty in turning Jack down, Beth spoke about The Beeches' problems to her close friend Isabel de Gines, who advised, 'What you need is a hero. What about your African Geordie?' Beth, realising that Isabel was right, retracted her decision and offered Jack the job, with the chance to become a partner after a six-month trial period. When Sandy visited Cardale and tried to dissuade Jack from staying, he made it clear that he saw his future there. Before leaving him for good, Sandy dubbed him 'a middle-aged Peter Pan terrified of growing up'.

Melanie Thaw played Kevin Whately's girl-friend in Peak Practice *after he acted her stepfa-ther John Thaw's side-kick in* Inspector Morse.

POWER LINES TRAGEDY

Beth and Jack had actually met before his unsuccessful first interview. As the aspiring country GP drove towards the village, late for his appointment following a breakdown on the motorway, he spotted Beth, who had just arrived at the scene of a tragedy. Two local boys, Rob Barnes and Paul Elliott, had been electrocuted as they tried to retrieve a kite entangled in power lines.

Stopping his car, Jack rushed to Paul – who had died instantly – while Beth treated Rob, who died later in hospital. Jack could only watch helplessly as Beth wept and cradled the dead boy in her arms. 'Leave her,' warned Will, who had just arrived. 'She delivered him.'

Ted and Sue Barnes blamed Paul for the death of their son, and 15-year-old Jazz Elliott – Paul's sister – blamed them for banning the two boys from seeing one another outside school, with the result that they met by playing truant. Jack tried to console Ted Barnes at The Manor Hotel but received a punch in the face for his trouble.

When Jazz smashed the Barnes' car windscreen and, knife in hand, ran amok in their immaculately tidy home, Sue revealed to the teenager the shocking news that she was really her husband Ted's secret love child. Jazz ran away but was tracked down by Jack, who persuaded her to return home and put the past behind her.

SETTLING IN

Temporarily ensconced at The Manor Hotel, run by James and Chloë White, until he could buy a place of his own, Jack soon settled in Cardale. But he got off to a bad start with practice nurse Ellie Ndebala

- The role of father Dave Elliott, whose son Paul died of electrocution after trying to retrieve a kite from power lines, was good practice for **Paul Broughton**, who subsequently played trade unionist Eddie Banks in *Brookside*, trying to cope with two tearaway sons.

Before entering acting, Paul worked in a variety of jobs, from bingo caller to golf caddie, and boxed as an amateur. He has also been seen in *The Bill*, *Between the Lines*, *Minder*, *Casualty* and *Cadfael*.

Rebecca Callard, daughter of *Coronation Street's* Beverley (Liz McDonald), made her name as Arrietty in two series of *The Borrowers* before playing Jazz Elliott, who had been brought up by Dave Elliott but was revealed to be Ted Barnes's secret child.

She has since acted Vicky in *September Song*, a teenage prostitute, Tula, in *Band of Gold*, chambermaid Kate Morris in *The Grand* and Harriet Marsh in *Plotlands*.

when he dressed a patient's leg ulcer without consulting her. She did not warm to his manner and felt he regarded her like one of his 'native trainees' at the Dry River Clinic. But it was not long before a little Kerruish charm resolved the situation and the two became firm friends.

Jack was quick to take The Beeches in hand. He warned Beth that, faced with competition from the new Brompton Health Centre, the practice must modernise. As a result, a new computer system was installed and receptionist Kim Beardsmore was made practice manager. There was also a new treatment room and a minor ops clinic. When lazy Will criticised Jack, Beth retorted, 'He's done more for the practice in two months than we have in years.'

BONKING BANK MANAGER

Bank manager Trevor Sharp, who had already been persuaded to freeze The Beeches' overdraft by scheming Dr John Reginald at the new health centre, showed little inclination to give the practice a loan when Jack presented him with his plans for refurbishment. But Jack was able to exert pressure on Trevor after catching him out during one of his fantasy sessions with hairdresser girlfriend Leanda in an upstairs room at The Manor Hotel.

Dressed as a cowboy and standing on top of the wardrobe, ready to pounce on his lover, who was handcuffed to the bed below, Trevor fell through the locked piece of furniture, leaving both him and the luscious Leanda trapped. Jack heard Leanda's screams and came to the rescue, called for an ambulance and, as Trevor was about to leave for hospital, offered him the loan application form, which the sheepish bank manager duly signed.

ANOTHER BATTLE FOR DOUGLAS

When Cardale's Battle of Britain ace and retired solicitor, Douglas Hart, started losing his sight because of cataracts, practice nurse Ellie Ndebala put pressure on the doctors at The Beeches to do something. She felt angry that his son, Ian, did not do more to help his father. Jack and Beth faced a dilemma when they suspected that patients at fundholding practices were getting operations quicker.

On a visit home, Ian Hart discovered his father had collapsed and, although only cold and confused, he was admitted to hospital. To Jack's anger, he was quickly discharged because his bed was needed for someone else. Alone at home, deciding he would rather be dead than become a burden, Douglas took a drugs overdose. Fortunately, he was still alive in the morning when Ellie made a visit. After being rushed to hospital, Douglas was told that he would still have to wait for an eye operation. However, when an incensed Jack and Ian confronted the consultant, he agreed to perform the operation in four weeks' time.

- Acting sexy Leanda in *Peak Practice*, who played out bank manager boyfriend Trevor Sharp's fantasies, was **Beth Goddard**, who went on to star as Dr Anna Pearce in *Degrees of Error*, Kelly Logan in *Ellington*, Cassandra in *BUGS*, Wendy in *Sunnyside Farm* and Suzanne de Tourney in *The Scarlet Pimpernel*.

Shaun Prendergast, who acted Trevor, has guest-starred in many television series, including *Waiting for God*, *Soldier Soldier*, *The Bill*, *Our Friends in the North*, *Between the Lines*, *Men of the World*, *Pie in the Sky*, *The Vanishing Man* and *Thief Takers*, as well as appearing in the films *Henry V* and *Mary Shelley's Frankenstein*.

- Veteran actor **Maurice Denham** played Douglas Hart, the Battle of Britain fighter pilot who had to wait for an operation after his eyesight was damaged by cataracts. Maurice, who started off as a comedy actor in classic radio series such as *ITMA* and *Much-Binding-in-the-Marsh*, has appeared in more than 100 feature films. He voiced all the animals in the 1954 animated version of George Orwell's political fable *Animal Farm*.

War veteran
Douglas Hart
(Maurice
Denham) finds
support from
Alice North
(Margery
Mason) when
he needs an
operation to
remove
cataracts.

WILL UNDER THREAT AT WORK...

Will Preston felt threatened by Jack, whom he sarcastically nicknamed 'Superman'. Will's acquisitive wife, Sarah, stirred up trouble by claiming that Will was being left to do all the 'donkey work' while Jack and Beth made the decisions.

When Beth informed Will that she planned to make Jack a partner, he saw red. 'He came here, he saw a lonely, vulnerable, single senior partner, and he set about making this place his own,' claimed a furious Will.

Will's initial antagonism towards Jack was not to last, and by the end of the year, Jack and Will had become good friends and business partners. Jack no longer represented a threat and, even more importantly, Jack offered Will care and support as he coped with the depression brought on by his crumbling marriage.

...AND ON THE ROCKS AT HOME

Will Preston (Simon Shepherd) finds that the aspirations of wife Sarah (Jacqueline Leonard) threaten the family's finances and his own lack of ambition.

Will could never earn enough money for Sarah. She wanted it all – skiing holidays, a flash house and a partnership for Will at the new health centre. But Will insisted that, even if John Reginald offered him a partnership, he was not sure whether he would take it. So he was devastated when he discovered that Sarah had embarked on an affair with Dr Daniel Acres in a calculated attempt to secure her ambitions for him. The liaison ended when Will rounded on Acres at a village event and snarled at the squirming doctor, 'If I so much as see you smile at Sarah again, I'll push all your teeth down your throat.'

Sarah and Will's marriage returned to a semblance of normality – but Will was banned from the marital bed. Eventually the strain became too much for Will and he developed reactive depression (depression brought on by external circumstances). Meanwhile, Sarah confided in Jack that she knew she was hurting Will but that she could not stop herself.

RUNNING INTO TROUBLE

Alan Sinclair (Bill Nighy) pushes athlete daughter Gemma (Natalie Morse) too hard as wife Maureen (Frances Low) looks on.

Budding young athlete Gemma Sinclair was fiercely driven by her overambitious father, Alan, whose own running career ended when he became crippled by rheumatoid arthritis. He could now live out his dreams only through his daughter, and winning meant everything to him.

When Gemma injured her knee while training, the teenager's mother, Maureen, was terrified that she would also develop arthritis. Jack came up against Alan's wrath when he advised against Gemma running in the forthcoming cross-country championships. Following a home visit from Jack, Gemma became smitten with him.

Later, Jack was horrified to see Gemma waiting at The Manor Hotel for him, fully made-up and all smiles. He drove the girl home and tried to let her down gently, but Gemma insisted that Jack make love to her and planted a kiss on his lips, an event witnessed by Sarah Preston as she made her way home after a rendevouz with her lover, Dr Daniel Acres.

When Gemma lied to her father, claiming that Jack had

- **Bill Nighy** played Alan Sinclair, who pushed his athlete daughter too hard in his quest to live out his dreams through her after his own running career had been cut short by rheumatoid arthritis.

  The actor had previously played an unfaithful university lecturer in *The Men's Room*, as well as appearing in series such as *Reilly – Ace of Spies*, *The Last Place on Earth*, *Bergerac*, the mini-series

Mistress of Suspense and many television plays.

Bill has since acted David Cleeve in the detective series *Wycliffe* and Mark Gordon in the prison series *Insiders*, also by *Peak Practice* creator Lucy Gannon. His real-life partner is actress Diana Quick.

• The role of farm labourer Ray Mason, who suffered from Raynauld's disease and found it difficult to put in the extra work needed to earn enough money to allow his infertile wife Val to have in vitro fertilisation treatment, was taken by **Wayne Foskett**. The actor had previously appeared in mini-series such as *Framed* and *Love and Reason*, and has since been seen in *Harry, Thief Takers, No Bananas* and *Noah's Ark*, as well as playing Keith in the series *Blind Men*.

said he loved her and that she would never run again, a furious Alan threatened to have Jack struck off. Fortunately for Jack, he was able to deliver to the family the news that Gemma's blood tests were negative. Free to take part in the cross-country race, Gemma apologised to Jack and told her father the truth. He withdrew his accusations and the young athlete went on to claim victory in the cross-country race.

KICKED WHEN DOWN

Val Mason and her farm labourer husband, Ray, were desperate to have a baby. Val accepted that, like her sister, Chloë White, she had difficulties in conceiving, but even so she was shocked to find out that she was suffering from cysted ovaries. In vitro fertilisation treatment, done privately at a cost of £800 per attempt, was her only chance of having a baby. Will advised Val to try twice and come to terms with a childless future if the procedure was unsuccessful.

Ray planned to work overtime to pay for the treatment – but nursed the painful secret that he was suffering from Raynauld's disease, an incurable circulatory condition that made doing his job difficult.

When, hardly able to operate his tractor, Ray crashed and broke his collar bone, ribs and an arm, he was rushed to hospital. Worse was to come when, as a result of his condition, his boss, Ken Waight, threw him out of his job and tied cottage. But golfing GP Will came to the rescue by persuading his club secretary to take on Ray as an odd-job man, with a tied cottage. The couple had a new house and renewed hoped that they could start a family.

MERRY WIDOW'S ROMANCE

When Cardale's merry widow, Isabel de Gines, decided she was ready for a romantic fling, she set her cap at quiet widower Gerard. Isabel told Gerard that she was fed up with being boring and would like a romance – a revelation that sent him scuttling away to think, leaving Isabel feeling embarrassed and awkward. The following day, Gerard – a very private man – invited Isabel for a walk and told her that he was interested but that he wanted their relationship to be kept quiet. As Isabel smiled and ran playfully towards a lovers' gate, she trod on a broken bottle that punctured her wellington boot.

Gerard accompanied her to The Beeches, where she was treated by Will in the new minor ops clinic. As Gerard waited in reception, Kim gave him a drink and teased him about chasing young girls through lovers' gates. The old man, mortified at being the butt of such jests, hurried away out of the surgery and Isabel's life.

PRIEST'S LESSON IN LIFE

Ponytailed Father Mel Daley was Cardale's Catholic priest with attitude. Dedicated to his duties as a local youth leader and parish priest, he carried a heavy workload. When Jack was called out after Mel cut his hand badly while preparing a meal for his housekeeper, Marjorie, and Isabel de Gines, he learned that this was Mel's third accident that week.

An accident occurred when Mel was knocked over by a Land Rover after being told by Bishop Stirland to make sure there was 'more theology and less politics' in his youth work. Mel confessed to a colleague, Father Clement Jennings, that he was terrified he was losing his mind.

Eventually he told Jack of his secret dread and of the headaches he had been experiencing. A neurologist discovered that the priest suffered from epilepsy. Despite assurances from Jack that it could be controlled with drugs, Mel was devastated. He regarded the condition as a form of mental illness and feared for his job at the youth centre. Mel tried to ignore the problem but was made to face up to it after suffering a fit during morning mass. When the priest had another, more severe, fit at the youth centre, distressed teenagers looked on in horror.

Mel took off into the Peaks to the site of a Celtic monument, searching for answers to his problem. Jack tracked Mel down and helped him to face up to his fears. 'If you, a priest, can't handle it, who can?' the GP challenged the unhappy priest. The turning point came when Mel saw

● **John Lynch**, who made his first screen impact as Helen Mirren's lover in the film *Cal*, played Roman Catholic priest Mel Daley, who feared for his job at a youth centre when he was diagnosed with epilepsy.

On TV, John played a Manchester United football star called Gavin, who fell for an electronics factory worker, in *Making Out*, and Peter Carson in *Chimera*. His other films include *The Secret Garden*, *In the Name of the Father*, *Some Mother's Son*, *Moll Flanders* and *Sliding Doors*.

The priest's housekeeper was played by **Tilly Vosburgh**, who had previously acted Mum in *Teenage Health Freak* and Jools Legge in *Full Stretch*. She has since become best known as Susan Rose in *EastEnders*.

that it was his fear of being seen as less than perfect that lay at the root of his difficulties. Able to face the community once again, he talked openly of his epilepsy during a warmly received sermon at morning mass.

• The inclusion of epilepsy in *Peak Practice* was, for Kevin Whately, an example of how television can help society. 'There was a girl who had an epileptic fit two days after the episode was screened,' he revealed. 'But her boyfriend had seen the episode and was able to help her. It's important for us to feature that sort of illness, because people can feel very isolated if they're not aware just how many others are in the same boat.'

FAULTY DIAGNOSIS

Fresh out of hospital after a bout of pleurisy, 82-year-old Hilda Lyons was busy ploughing a field when Beth paid her a visit. The octogenarian insisted that she was fighting fit, but Beth was called back when Hilda fell and grazed her face while repairing a dry-stone wall.

Despite Beth's warnings, Hilda insisted on working, only to collapse again. This time, Dr Rhiann Lewis – a trainee GP at the health centre – was sent to help, but she

• Before playing Det. Insp. Sally Johnson in *The Bill*, actress **Jaye Griffiths** tried to steal Jack Kerruish's heart in *Peak Practice* as motorbiking Dr Rhiann Lewis, who was seen in two episodes as a trainee at the rival health centre.

In real life, the actress once had ambitions to care for animals. 'I dearly wanted to be a vet,' she says. 'But, unfortunately, physics was not a subject that came naturally to me and I knew I wouldn't get the necessary qualifications.'

Deciding on acting as a career, her first job on leaving drama school was at the Chichester Festival Theatre, where she spent six months brushing Diana Rigg's hair. She also trod the professional boards for the first time as one of Cleopatra's maids in *Antony and Cleopatra*. Before her role in *Peak Practice*, Jaye had appeared as journalist Molly Cope in *Between the Lines*. She has also starred as Laverne in one series of *Love Hurts*, Ros in *BUGS* and Tanya in *Unfinished Business*.

Elaine Donnelly, who was Gordon Clegg's wife-to-be, Caroline Wilson, in *Coronation Street* in 1982, acted Liz Barber, neighbour of 82-year-old Hilda Lyons whom Dr Rhiann Lewis misdiagnosed as having meningitis. She subsequently acted Ivy Collins in *No Bananas* and has appeared in *Dangerfield* and *The Locksmith*.

Dr Rhiann Lewis (Jaye Griffiths) rides into Cardale – and briefly into Jack's life – but falls foul of Beth when she makes a wrong diagnosis.

mistook Hilda's symptoms for meningitis and sent her to hospital. On finding out, Beth complained to Jack about Rhiann's actions but, to her dismay, he defended the trainee, with whom he had enjoyed a fling. In turn, Rhiann felt that Beth was overreacting and jealous of her involvement with Jack.

JACK AND BETH'S CHEMISTRY

There was a powerful attraction between Jack and Beth from the minute they met. Though they fought hard to deny their feelings for one another – they had both been hurt in the past, Jack in his marriage and subsequent relationship with Sandy, and Beth in an affair with her married former boss, Dr Michael Cummings – it was impossible. Not even Jack's dalliance with Rhiann Lewis could quash their budding romance.

Beth had never met anyone like Jack before. He raced through her life like a whirlwind, bursting with fresh ideas and enthusiasm. But the pair often clashed when difficulties arose – Jack's style was to meet problems head on, whereas Beth took a softly, softly approach. Although they were spending more and more time together and Jack had given Beth the key to his new cottage, Beth preferred to keep their relationship a secret. This sometimes led to near-farcical situations, such as the time when practice manager Kim saw Beth dropping Jack off in a country lane so that they wouldn't arrive together at work.

JACK FIGHTS FOR EQUALITY

When Francis Barrat collapsed with a heart attack after 18 months of heart trouble, Jack sprang into action and rushed him to hospital, giving him cardiac massage and mouth-to-mouth resuscitation on the way when he stopped breathing. Jack discovered that despite the severity of his condition, he was not on a list for an operation. Francis's ex-miner friend Danny Jackson explained that this was probably because Francis's consultant had put him on medication only and Francis was frightened to make a fuss.

• **Sean Pertwee**, son of the late *Doctor Who* and *Worzel Gummidge* TV star Jon, switched from villain to victim to play Francis Barrat, who suffered heart trouble but who had to wait for treatment. He had just finished shooting his role in the ram-raiding film *Shopping* alongside Sean Bean.

Shooting an episode of *Peak Practice* also enabled Sean to be reunited with Simon Shepherd, who had appeared with him in the Central Television series *Chancer*. Sean has since played Hugh Beringar in *Cadfael* and Ian Worrell in *Bodyguards*, as well as acting in the films *Blue Juice* and *Stiff Upper Lip*.

In *Peak Practice*, Sean's character, Francis, was given the kiss of life by Kevin Whately. This experience was made worse by the fact that Francis had to be seen being sick, with soup being used for the vomiting scenes.

The role of Francis's friend Danny Jackson was taken by **Chris Walker**, who many viewers remembered as PC Nick Shaw in early series of *The Bill*, Brian Rimmer in *The Manageress* and the hapless Sergeant Wallis in a series of BT commercials – a spoof of Kevin Whately's role as Sgt Lewis in *Inspector Morse*

Consultant cardiologist Dr Laurence Reeve explained to Jack that Francis had not been considered for surgery because resources were to be used only for those with a good chance of survival. Francis did not have this, so drugs were more appropriate. Jack disagreed and encouraged Francis's mother, Rita, and Danny to push for the operation to be done privately, at a cost of about £5,000. Danny hoped that some of the money would come from the miners' social fund. Jack and Will took part in a fundraising run through Cardale, which helped to bring in enough money for the operation.

Francis was admitted to hospital and Jack waited anxiously for news. When it came, he was devastated. Although the operation had gone well, Francis never regained consciousness. 'At least you cared enough to try,' comforted Beth as Jack berated himself for raising everyone's hopes.

alongside Mel Smith taking off Morse.

Chris subsequently acted Det. Chief Insp. Paul Boyd in *Our Friends in the North*, Lord Athelstone in *Ivanhoe*, corrupt footballer Bronco Layne in *The Fix*, Matthew Mullen in *Playing the Field* and Fred Stephens in *Sunny's Ears*. He also acted Ray Thorpe in *Coronation Street*, who was the boyfriend of Tricia Armstrong, played by Tracy Brabin, who is the real-life partner of *Peak Practice* star Richard Platt.

Other noted character players in the same episode of *Peak Practice* included **Anne Reid** – best known as Ken Barlow's first wife, Valerie, in *Coronation Street* – in the role of Francis's wife, Rita; **Benjamin Whitrow**, later to act Mr Bennet in *Pride and Prejudice*, as Dr Laurence Reeve; and **Caroline Langrishe**, noted for her appearances as Kate Pulaski in writer Roy Clarke's satirical crime series *Pulaski* and Carol in *The Return of Shelley*, as Dr Susan Lees.

WILL'S MONEY-MAKING DECEPTION

Will Preston was a man cracking under the weight of an unhappy marriage and a salary that was insufficient to support his wife's demanding lifestyle. As debts piled up, Sarah suffered the humiliation of having a cheque dishonoured at the village store and son Tony bringing home a school fees reminder.

Will found a way of making more money by taking part in a drugs trial, monitoring the effects of anti-inflammatories on 25 of his patients for a large pharmaceutical company. He decided not to tell his partners, knowing that Beth in particular disapproved of using patients in this way. Will conducted the tests himself, but failed to update participating patients' consultation notes. After half the patients dropped out, in desperation Will started to fabricate test results.

When elderly Alice North, one of Will's guinea pigs, began to suffer from severe abdominal pain, she was examined by Beth despite her protests that she must see only Will. Alice's husband had died from stomach cancer and she was terrified that she would meet the same fate. Unable to face up to her fears, she kept the pains from Will. Then Alice's pain became more severe, and she began to vomit and developed jaundice. Jack listened as Alice explained that she thought Will was keeping the truth – that she had stomach cancer – from her. She added that he saw her every week and gave her 'some special drugs from his cupboard'. Jack assured Alice that she was suffering from gall bladder problems and called an ambulance to take her to hospital, where she made a full recovery after a successful operation.

With his clandestine activities out in the open, Will confessed to Beth and Jack that he had made up Alice's results. 'I've certainly lost any respect I had for you,' Beth shouted at a contrite Will as he tried in vain to apologise. Although Beth wanted Will to leave, Jack felt that she was writing him off too quickly and that they should try to help him. At the same time, Will's wife, Sarah, threatened to walk out on him if he left the practice.

As Will slipped deeper into depression, events came to a head when Sarah told Will that she had returned the new car that he had bought her to the dealer and said he had no 'backbone'. Will flipped and as he went on a rampage through the house, wrecking everything in his path, Beth was called. Holding Will as he wept bitterly, Beth admitted that she was wrong. Will did need help – and time off to deal with his depression.

JACK TO THE RESCUE

Jack's abilities as the newest member of the local mountain rescue team were put to the test when a young man with suspected kidney failure – Ian Hilliard – was stranded, unconscious, on Curbar Gap, high in the Peaks.

Earlier, when Ian and his fiancée, Marie, went white-water canoeing with their friend Paul in preparation for an adventure holiday, Ian had to be dragged to safety after his canoe capsized, following a bout of vomiting that morning. He now needed a medical check and fitness certificate to get insurance for the holiday in the Peaks. Ian revealed to Beth that he had been given a kidney transplant five years earlier and, alarmed at finding traces of blood and albumen in his urine sample, she referred him to a renal unit.

Instead of going to the hospital, Ian concealed his illness from Marie and Paul, packed his camping gear and made his way with Paul to Curbar Gap, a bleak and rocky spot. As they struggled over the rugged terrain, the weather conditions worsened and the friends pitched their tent for the night. The following morning, Paul discovered Ian unconscious and ran for help. In his hurry to do so, he fell and

• Kevin Whately and his actress wife, **Madelaine Newton**, appeared in their fourth different programme together when she acted in the last episode of *Peak Practice*'s first series. He had played a miner in *When the Boat Comes In*, in which Madelaine played James Bolam's girlfriend. She then guest-starred in Kevin's two previous TV hits, *Auf Wiedersehen Pet* and *Inspector Morse*, both made by Central Television.

In *Peak Practice*, Madelaine played Kevin's instructor, Irene, who put Jack to the test when he sought to expand his medical knowledge by joining a mountain rescue team. He soon had to put the theory into practice when a kidney transplant patient was lost in the mountains as a storm brewed.

'We shot the scenes in the Peak District National Park, which is one of the most beautiful areas of the Peaks,' recalls Kevin. 'It was nice to share with Madelaine some of what had been keeping me away from her and the kids.'

Madelaine was, in fact, a face known to millions of TV viewers before Kevin shot to fame. She had acted in all three series of *When the Boat Comes In* and has more recently been seen in *Catherine Cookson's The*

broke a leg.

The mountain rescue team, with Jack, found Paul, who was unable to give them clear directions to Ian. To Jack's relief, the team spotted Ian's green tent in the nick of time. Ian was winched into a helicopter and flown straight to hospital, where he was put on a dialysis machine. As weather conditions deteriorated, Jack made his way down the mountainside and home to bed, where he collapsed into a well-deserved deep sleep, totally exhausted.

Cinder Path and in *Coronation Street*, in which she played Mary McKenna, mother of Fiona Middleton's ex-fiancé, Alan.

Sean Gallagher, who acted Ian Hilliard, the irresponsible kidney transplant patient taking to the mountains, went on to appear on TV as Ray Barker in *The House of Windsor* and Alan in *Holding On*. He also acted alongside Amanda Burton once more in *Silent Witness*.

In *Peak Practice*, his fiancée, Marie, was played by **Jayne Ashbourne**, great-granddaughter of one of the original Black and White Minstrels. She had already filmed one series of *The Riff Raff Element*, in which she acted Carmen, and went on to appear as Sarah Madson in *Madson*, Carol's half-sister, Lisa, in *Gold* and William Palmer's wife, Annie, in *The Life and Crimes of William Palmer*.

COUPLE'S DREAM COMES TRUE

The Manor Hotel hosts Chloë and James White had tried for a child for many years, but it was not until Chloë was given fertility treatment that their dream came true. Baby Sarah-Jane was born four weeks early at Merry Cottage, a local holiday home where James had insisted Chloë stayed in an effort to make her rest. She was delivered by Beth and Will, with James watching on until it all became too much for him and the anxious new father keeled over.

It's all smiles behind The Manor Hotel bar for James and Chloë White (Richard Platt and Hazel Ellerby) when fertility treatment results in daughter Sarah-Jane's birth after years of trying for children.

HOPE FOR WILL

Battling with depression, Will had spent his days sitting aimlessly in front of the television until Beth called him to help at the birth of Sarah-Jane. As he sprang into action and dashed off into the night, he showed a little of his old spark. On his return, Will found that Sarah had waited up for him. She invited him in to their bed and, as he poured them each a brandy, he was left with new hope for their marriage.

JACK'S PRIDE AND JOY

One of Dr Jack Kerruish's trade-marks on his rounds in *Peak Practice* was his elegant, two-litre, silver-grey, four-seater Bristol 405, one of only 1,000 manufactured by the firm in the fifties.

He followed in a line of television characters with distinctive classic cars that included Bergerac in his open-roofed Riley and Morse in his Jaguar Mk II.

But actor Kevin Whately almost ended up with an entirely different motor. He himself liked the idea of a Volvo while producer Tony Virgo wanted an Alfa Romeo. Their minds were made up when Tony and Gordon Flemyng, who directed the first two episodes, spotted the Bristol near Marble Arch, around the corner from Central Television's London offices in Portman Square — but not before another car had been bought.

'Originally, we went out and bought a Reliant Scimitar going back to the seventies, like the one Princess Anne had,' recalls chief production buyer John Steppings. 'Then, when I met Gordon Flemyng and Tony Virgo in London, they were returning from lunch and spotted a Bristol car parked next to the kerb.

'They asked me to see whether I could get hold of it, so I found out who owned it from a parking attendant, knocked on the door of the owner and started negotiating for it. We started off at about £8,000 and we ended up at £12,000, but it was worth every penny. I bought it, took the keys and drove the car back to the Nottingham studios.

'The idea was that the car had to look old because it had been in storage while Jack was in Africa. What we wanted was a car that looked very old, and the silver-grey colour was all warm. Later, we had to replace the gearbox and it took a lot of money to keep it on the road for three series.'

The Bristol, launched at the 1954 Paris Motor Show and nicknamed 'The Flying Greenhouse' for its swift performance and steeply raked rear screen, was bought from Geoffrey Herdman, treasurer of the Bristol Owners' Club, who purchased the car at an auction in 1985.

WHAT THE PAPERS SAID

'The pre-launch poster campaign seemed to promise *All Creatures Great and Small* with added *Morse* appeal, but the reality is more interesting. Kevin Whately, whose main function until now was to ask Morse dumb questions, had those who doubted his ability to carry a series. But he can and has, as the complex (that is, he can suggest more than two emotions at once — and if you think that's easy look at the difficulty hard John Thaw has in expressing just one) and believable Dr Jack Kerruish.'

The Independent

KEVIN WHATELY
as Dr Jack Kerruish

Leaving his role as Inspector Morse's sidekick after seven years, Kevin Whately stepped into *Peak Practice* as its star and quickly made the idealistic Dr Jack Kerruish one of television's best-loved characters.

It also gave him his first screen kiss for many years, when Jack was seen returning to girlfriend Sandy after his halcyon days building up a new clinic in Africa. Sandy soon found herself cast aside as Jack ploughed himself into The Beeches surgery in rural Derbyshire and fell for senior partner Beth Glover.

But the sizzling scenes between Jack and Beth were tempered by the freezing temperatures during filming of the first series. 'We deliberately opted to shoot in the winter to capture the bleakness of rural life,' recalls Kevin. 'It was a bit of a shock because we always filmed *Morse* in the summer.'

It was also a shock for some viewers to come to terms with the transformation from Kevin's short-back-and-sides image as Sgt Lewis in *Inspector Morse* to long hair and button-down shirts in his role of an unconventional GP. 'Playing a dynamic character like Dr Kerruish after someone who just stands there being told "Go on, Lewis" all the time is wonderfully liberating,' says Kevin.

Being thrust into the spotlight made Kevin one of the hottest properties in television – and a sex symbol. 'I'm amazed at people's taste in actors,' he says, modestly. 'I'm a very reluctant sex symbol.'

The actor researched the role of Jack by spending time with doctors at a surgery near his home in Bedfordshire, which he shares with his actress wife, Madelaine Newton, and their two children, Kitty and Kieran. Madelaine actually appeared in the final episode of the first series as a mountain rescue ranger.

Filming in the Peak District brought back memories of the Northeast countryside that Kevin enjoyed as a child. Born in Northumberland, the son of a sailor, he toyed with becoming a doctor, but – deterred by the long time it would take to qualify – trained as an accountant and

joined top firm Price Waterhouse. He left after three years to study acting at the Central School of Speech and Drama in London and supported himself by busking on the Underground, which resulted in him being arrested twice. His talent for playing the guitar had already found an outlet when he teamed up with friend Andy McKay to form a folk duo, touring pubs and clubs in Ireland before getting exposure back home on the BBC regional programme *Look North*.

After drama school, Kevin made one of his earliest television appearances, as a miner in *When the Boat Comes In* – in which he acted alongside his wife-to-be – and briefly played a lorry driver in *Coronation Street* in 1981. He then found fame as naïve brickie Neville in the hit series *Auf Wiedersehen Pet*. Before landing the role of Sgt Lewis in *Inspector Morse,* he had played a police constable in *Juliet Bravo* and another detective sergeant in *A Murder Is Announced* in the BBC's 'Miss Marple' series.

Since leaving *Peak Practice*, Kevin has acted as a wife batterer in Lucy Gannon's one-off TV drama *Trip Trap*, returned to his role as Lewis in several *Inspector Morse* specials and starred as detective-turned-insurance investigator Jimmy Griffin in the series *The Broker's Man*.

He still enjoys going back to Northumberland with his wife and children when he has time off. 'We usually stay with Madelaine's sister, who is married to a farmer and lives in a remote, tough area in the Cheviot hills,' he explains. 'It's a hard life, working the land but, for us, as visitors, it's an idyllic world with lots of animals for the kids to enjoy, and good food and talk around the big kitchen table. It's just the kind of life I love.'

AMANDA BURTON

as Dr Beth Glover

Playing glamorous accountant Heather Haversham in *Brookside* during the eighties brought Amanda Burton a legion of fans and the title of the sexiest star in soaps. But the late director Gordon Flemyng, who spotted her potential for the role of Dr Beth Glover in *Peak Practice*, advised the actress to dress down for her audition so that she would avoid looking *too* glamorous as the more down-to-earth GP tramping around the Derbyshire countryside.

'The first thing that attracted me to the

role was her strength of character,' says Amanda. 'I like the fact that she is very much her own woman. I liked her independence. It's something I have. I could never imagine playing a character who isn't strong.'

Being seen as a sex symbol is, to Amanda, simply a bonus to acting roles that meet with her approval. 'I've never played any deeply sexy roles, yet I am seen as a sex symbol some of the time,' she says. 'I find that contradictory when you think about the work I've done, but I'm not complaining.'

Londonderry-born Amanda, whose parents acted in amateur plays, trained at the Manchester Polytechnic School of Theatre. She had a few small television roles before joining *Brookside*'s original cast in 1982 as half of yuppie couple Roger and Heather Huntington. When solicitor husband Roger cheated on her, they split up, but Amanda carried on in the Channel Four serial until leaving in 1986.

Two years later, she was reaching bigger audiences when she took the role of Michael Elphick's sidekick, Margaret Daly, in one series of *Boon*. Appearances followed in *Inspector Morse*, *Van Der Valk*, *Stay Lucky* and *Lovejoy* until, after playing a solicitor in *Minder*, she landed the role of Dr Beth Glover in *Peak Practice*.

She was remembered by Gordon Flemyng, who directed her in *Minder* and thought her perfect for the part, and *Peak Practice* script editor Julian Murphy had worked with her on *Boon*. The actress herself felt it apt that she was finally to play a doctor on television. 'I've always been interested in medicine since I was little,' she says. 'I did an odd combination for A-levels – literature and biology.'

Amanda researched her new role by sitting in on some of her own GP's surgeries. 'I saw about 18 patients, who all had vastly different problems,' she recalls. 'He dealt with each one quite differently and showed a very good personal touch.'

Playing Beth gave Amanda something to get her teeth into as an actress. 'Some aspects of this job can be a bit like a cattle market and I try to avoid that,' she says. 'I don't want to be playing roles that are just there for some love interest. What attracts me are roles which are raw and emotional. I was moved by the opening episode of *Peak Practice* when two boys were killed after touching electric cables. And I've read scripts which made me cry.'

Starring in *Peak Practice* also elevated Amanda to the top rung of the television ladder. Not surprisingly, after three series, Amanda was lured away by the chance to play forensic pathologist Dr Sam Ryan, the sole star, in three series of *Silent Witness*. During her last year in *Peak Practice*, the actress – who with her second husband, celebrity photographer Sven Arnstein, has two daughters, Phoebe and Brid – was rocked by newspaper allegations of a romance with co-star Kevin Whately. 'I've never spoken about that and never will,' says Amanda. 'I left *Peak Practice* because I was offered the role in *Silent Witness*. Three years on one series was enough and I had a fantastic lead part on a BBC series to go to.'

Amanda met Sven when he took publicity pictures of her on the *Brookside* set. They eventually married in 1989 and the actress found time to give birth to her two daughters. 'Having children has changed me,' she says. 'It's made me grow up more and made me think less about myself. Since I've had my children, I've also found that I have huge amounts of energy. I have great fun with my daughters. We do lots of silly voices and dance together. I like to make the best of the time that I have with them.'

SIMON SHEPHERD

as Dr Will Preston

Playing Dr Will Preston in *Peak Practice*, who suffers marriage problems and has a breakdown, made Simon Shepherd a household name. The downhill spiral of television's most handsome GP was a shock to those who watched avidly, but Simon loved having a role to get his teeth into.

'Many viewers were taken aback by Dr Preston having a nervous breakdown,' he recalls. 'It was very graphic and it scared people to see a doctor – even if it's only a fictional character – cracking up before their eyes.'

At the height of Will's traumas, shopping at the supermarket became an ordeal as Simon was besieged by fans. 'People kept telling me I looked much better despite my breakdown and one lady asked if I was up to pushing my trolley,' he says.

Taking the role of Will, after playing upper-class cad Piers Garfield-Ward in the series *Chancer*, required Simon to look like an authentic country GP. But, being squeamish, he was not ideally suited to it.

'At the cinema, I can't look at any bloody scenes in case I faint,' says the actor. 'But, at the same time, I can't really look away. I often have to walk out of cinemas and theatres. I keep telling myself that it's only actors covered in blood and surrounded by camera and props. Even if I can see the "blood" pump working or the props man holding up the offal or the liver or whatever, I have difficulty.'

After his divorce, Will's final link with his wife, Sarah, and their two sons, Tony and Julian, disappeared when she took them to America. However, the doctor eventually found happiness with another GP, Kate Webster, although they left for Bristol after their baby daughter, Emily, was diagnosed with cystic fibrosis and she was given the chance of a better life by becoming part of a research programme in the city.

Will disappeared from *Peak Practice* in 1997 after Simon went on to play unorthodox scientist Sam Bliss in the ITV series *Bliss*. 'The opportunity to star in my own series coincided with my feelings that, after four series of *Peak Practice*, it was time to move on.' However, he returned for the first four episodes of the fifth series to give continuity and introduce a new doctor, David Shearer.

Becoming an actor was an early decision in Simon's life. Born in Bristol, the son of a publican, he was just three when his parents moved on to The Dirty Duck, in Stratford-upon-Avon, where they numbered members of the Royal Shakespeare Company among their regulars.

'I did go to the theatre from a very early age,' he recalls, 'so I was very aware of the theatrical event of a first night and also saw a lot of Shakespeare. In fact, it was quite a while before I even realised that there were other forms of theatre. Acting was the one thing at school that I was confident doing. That was my identity because I wasn't good at sports or particularly gifted academically. Acting was something I knew I could do and enjoyed doing.' After boarding at Clifton College, back in his former home city, Simon trained at the Bristol Old Vic Theatre School.

After years in the business, *Peak Practice* made Simon a star and, in between series, gave him the chance to act adulterous Captain Duncan McAllister, whose affair with a female soldier led to the tragic murder of his wife, in the TV crime-of-passion drama *Beyond Reason*. Simon admits that he related to the character because the opportunities for infidelity are common for actors. 'In this business, temptation is everywhere,' he says. 'You have to be in control or you'd go off the rails. You have to be very honest to yourself and the person you're with. Honesty is everything.'

In Simon's case, he has avoided temptation and enjoys a happy family life with his costume designer wife, Alexandra Byrne – who has worked on productions such as Jane Austen's *Persuasion* for television and Kenneth Branagh's film version of *Hamlet* – son Joe, twins Arthur and Billie, and youngest daughter Beatrice. The actor, who was 40 when he left *Peak Practice*, married at the age of 24 and always longs to return to his wife and children at their home near Bath after filming. 'Maybe I'm old-fashioned,' he says. 'But, as far as I'm concerned, you make a decision about who you want to be with and how you want to spend your life, and then you stick to it. I passionately believe in fidelity and commitment.'

1994

The biggest question in viewers' minds as *Peak Practice* began a second series was whether Jack and Beth's relationship would blossom. How Will recovered from his nervous breakdown and struggled to keep his family together as they downsized their life style was the other continuing theme throughout the series.

'I knew the characters so well by the time I sat down to work on the second series, it wrote itself,' recalls Lucy Gannon. 'The characters demanded that Jack and Beth held back. Jack was a very intense character who wanted to do right by everybody all the time and his ideals were always fighting with his testosterone. Beth was quite suspicious of him because he seemed to be so "right on" and together, and she didn't want to get involved, particularly not with a business partner. Also, Will had to get a real shake-up in this series.'

This time, with a new transmission day of Tuesday, there were 13 episodes – the first set six months after the end of the first series. The second series dealt with issues such as asthma, AIDS, abortion, faith healing, schizophrenia, euthanasia and the politics of practices becoming fundholders, something that Beth finally accepted, despite her concern that money was becoming more important than patients. 'I think altogether this year,' said Kevin Whately at the time, 'we have gone for more heavyweight subjects, which was what I wanted in the first place. It's all meaty stuff. The schizophrenia scenes were very emotional.'

Creator Lucy Gannon had planned the move into fundholding before the first series had even gone into production, not for political reasons but because the issue was becoming a reality. 'There is no politics in my scripts ever,' she insists, 'because I'm completely uncluttered. I'm free of that and wanted the series to be.

Kevin Whately, Amanda Burton and Simon Shepherd consolidated their popularity with the 1994 series which saw The Beeches become a fundholding practice.

So what we ended up with was a doctor who was very much against fundholding, a doctor who was for fundholding but for the wrong reasons, and a man stuck in the middle who knew they had to go into it for practical reasons.'

By now, *Peak Practice* had put the Derbyshire village of Crich firmly on the television map and The Manor Hotel, in nearby South Wingfield, was doing a roaring trade in T-shirts. The second series proved even more popular, attracting as many as 14.7 million viewers and gaining a regular spot in television's top ten programmes.

'The great thing about the second series,' recalls Lucy Gannon, 'was that I moved from Derby into the countryside, nearer to Belper, where the *Peak Practice* production office was situated. We were able to have brilliant script meetings that went on until two in the morning, with rafts of bottles of wine. It was such a friendly team and, because it was local to me, I got a tremendous amount of feedback from the public.'

THE CHARACTERS

DR JACK KERRUISH (Kevin Whately)
Settled into The Beeches and in a relationship with senior partner Dr Beth Glover, Jack still behaves like a bull in a china shop sometimes, but his sense of justice and concern for patients is commendable.

DR BETH GLOVER (Amanda Burton)
Although she has fallen for Jack's charms, Beth is unwilling to abandon her independence, which ensures a fiery relationship. At the surgery, she faces pressure to make The Beeches a fundholding practice.

DR WILL PRESTON (Simon Shepherd)
Recovering from a nervous breakdown after six months in a rehabilitation clinic, Will returns to The Beeches with renewed zeal and energy. He and his wife, Sarah, face eco-nomic realities by moving to a smaller house.

SARAH PRESTON (Jacqueline Leonard)
Trying to make a fresh start with husband Will, Sarah tries to patch up their marriage for the sake of their two sons. She gets a job as a school secretary and tries to accept the financial cutbacks that have proved to be necessary.

ISABEL DE GINES (Sylvia Syms)
Beth's lifelong friend continues to support Beth's involvement with Jack, both professionally and personally. Isabel herself briefly finds romance with local businessman Ken Alton.

KIM BEARDSMORE (Esther Coles)
Now receptionist *and* practice manager, Kim hopes to become fund manager when their new fundholding status comes into being – but is she the woman for the job?

ELLIE NDEBALA (Sharon Hinds)
Although standoffish, Ellie remains an efficient and professional practice nurse.

**JAMES and CHLOE WHITE
(Richard Platt and Hazel Ellerby)**
After years of trying for a family, The Manor Hotel owners James and Chloë were delighted with the birth of daughter Sarah-Jane. But James worries that Chloë might be suffering from postnatal depression.

ALICE NORTH (Margery Mason)
Pensioner Alice, who has a heart of gold, has survived a gall bladder operation and moved into Douglas Hart's home to look after him following his own cataract operation.

TREVOR SHARP (Shaun Prendergast)
Bank manager Trevor, who authorised a loan to The Beeches after being caught with his pants down by Jack, is still seeing girlfriend Leanda, but he has to face up to another potential problem in the bedroom.

LEANDA (Beth Goddard)
Hairdresser Leanda's on-off relationship with Trevor has survived an embarrassing sexual misadventure when their cowboy fantasy was discovered by Jack.

PROFITABLE PRACTICE

The Beeches came to grips with becoming a fund-holding practice, responsible for its own budgets, in 1994. The fictional Mid-Derbyshire Health Authority holds a sum of money agreed with the practice as the amount to be available annually for spending in four key areas, but – unlike non-fundholders – the practice decides where the money is best spent. The four areas are:

Drugs Budget The practice is allocated a sum of money to pay for all the drugs it prescribes to patients. This is strictly regulated and the doctors have to stay within budget. Hence the pressure to prescribe cheaper and older drugs. As a dispensing practice until 1998, The Beeches was paid for giving out drugs at about £1 per item.

Patient Services Emergency hospital admissions are free, but others cost the practice money. Minor operations, such as vasectomies and removal of lesions, save the practice money. Additionally, the GP who performs them at the surgery is paid extra money by the health authority, earning the practice extra income.

Staff Budget Apart from doctors' salaries, all medical staff, including practice nurses, have to be paid out of the fund, but profit can be made by, for example, hiring a physiotherapist to visit twice a week and renting out a room.

Management Allowance Office equipment and stationery is bought out of this budget.

The salaries of partners in the practice, who are self-employed and exempt from VAT, are paid from each GP's capitation allowance – the amount per patient paid by the health authority to each partner – and items of service payments such as immunisations, smears and antenatal care. This profit is then divided between the doctors to give an annual income of £40,000 to £50,000. So the move to fundholding gave The Beeches a strong incentive to run a profitable business.

Practice profits, and therefore GPs' salaries, can be further boosted by up to 30 per cent through dispensing drugs (which The Beeches did until having to close its dispensary in 1998 after Norman Shorthose's pharmacy opened in Cardale). Extra payment is available for hitting certain targets, and fixed-amount expenses are paid for fuel bills and the use of non-medical staff such as cleaners.

GPs can also earn money outside practice hours, offering medical services to local companies or working as clinical assistants to hospital doctors or medical advisers to the media. This has nothing to do with practice finances but can cause disagreement if it adversely affects a doctor's performance in the practice.

Fundholding will cease to exist from April 1999. The Beeches will have to co-operate more with other local practices to organise its patient care, with resources pooled from a primary care group fund. The aim is to give more equality to patients.

BETH REJECTS JACK

Beth became unsure about her relationship with Jack and sought time on her own. Although this confused Jack, he was more certain than ever that he wanted to make a commitment to her. However, she made it clear that she could not do the same when she turned down his proposal of marriage, adamant that she was 'not ready to bow out'. The couple's relationship then went through a frosty period.

PREACHER'S BLIND FAITH

When visiting preacher John Adams led a charismatic service at Cardale's parish church and challenged those who were ill to be healed by their faith alone, Anne, mother of young asthma sufferer Penny, took him at his word and stopped her daughter's medication, disillusioned with conventional medicine. Local pastor the Rev. Neil Winters told John that he was being irresponsible and simplifying matters.

When Penny next had an asthma attack, Anne hid her inhaler and called John round to pray. Penny's wheezing stopped, and Anne felt she had the proof she needed. Days later, her daughter was taken ill at school with asthma, but Anne refused to let Jack and nurse Ellie send her to hospital – despite Jack's warning that the girl would die if she did not receive help.

The GP, gravely concerned for his young patient, threatened to contact social services for an emergency order. Anne, terrified, asked John to lay hands on Penny. Sweating profusely and totally out of his depth, he pan-

• Rushing an asthma sufferer to hospital in his role as Jack Kerruish brought back unhappy memories for Kevin Whately. As a child, he also battled against the illness, which did not disappear completely until the actor was in his thirties.

'I used to fall over in a wheezing heap on the school field and I remember the feelings of pain and panic,' he recalled after filming the story.

The Rev. Neil Winters, who in the same episode rebuked a visiting preacher for telling his congregation that their ill-

nesses could be cured by faith alone, was played by **David Hargreaves**, an acclaimed Northern character actor with Royal Shakespeare Company stage experience.

On TV, he has acted Tom Darblay, husband of police inspector Jean, in three series of *Juliet Bravo*, market superintendent Derek Owen in every episode of the serial *Albion Market* and Arthur Scargill in the drama-documentary *The Miners' Strike*.

LEFT
Jack carries asthma sufferer Penny Meadows (Sara Cragg) away for treatment after her mother takes a visiting preacher's words on faith healing too literally.

• **Peter Armitage** took the role of Rob Clulow, a smoker in need of a bypass operation, before returning to *Coronation Street* as Kevin Webster's father, Bill, who had been seen earlier in the serial in the mid-eighties.

He has also acted David Jason's brother, Randolph Mepstead, in the sitcom *Lucky Feller* and Jim Butler in the detective series *Sam Saturday*, and played character roles in *Lovejoy*, *Parnell and the Englishwoman*,

icked and begged Anne to let Jack – who was beating on the front door – into the house. Once inside, Jack grabbed Penny and bundled her into his car to take her to hospital, despite Anne's efforts to stop him. Thanks to Jack's quick actions, Penny received life-saving treatment just in time.

BANK MANAGER LOSES INTEREST

Cardale's canoodling bank manager, Trevor Sharp, was worried when his sex life took a nose dive. Normally a twice-a-day man, Trevor was finding it difficult to rise to the occasion more than once or twice a week. His girl-friend Leanda's best attempts at seduction failed to improve matters.

After consulting Jack at The Beeches, Trevor realised that he was placing himself under too much stress. He agreed to be happy with what and who he was and, during a heart-to-heart chat with Leanda, asked the local hairdresser to be his wife. Trevor was over the moon when she said yes.

SURGEON STUBS OUT OPERATION

Quarry worker Rob Clulow was a single parent left to raise three children and hold down a full-time job after his wife walked out on him for another man. A heavy smoker, he also had a major heart problem, but hospital surgeon Dominic Jenkins refused to carry out a bypass operation until he quit his deadly habit. Will considered Rob's angina to be self-inflicted, but Beth and Jack were shocked by Jenkins's decision. Despite their individual efforts to persuade him to reconsider, they failed to make the surgeon change his mind.

When Will and wife Sarah moved to a smaller house in the area to save money, their son Tony struck up a friendship with Rob's 11-year-old son, Harry, who was being threatened by a gang of village bullies. When the pair were attacked by bricks, stones and wooden missiles as they sat on the window ledge of a disused mill, Tony retaliated by throwing a brick that missed its target, crashed through a glazed roof and sent daggers of glass onto one of the bullies below, severing an artery in the boy's leg. Fortunately, he recovered in hospital after a blood transfusion, but Tony was later taken to a police station with his parents and given a formal caution.

The incident left a marked impression on Will. 'You and Jack are right – people must come first,' he told Beth. Inspired by his newfound compassion, Will found a way during a game of golf with Jenkins to convince the surgeon that he should go ahead with a bypass operation for Rob, which was successful.

Jack the Ripper, G.B.H., Heartbeat, Medics, The Bill, Harry, Casualty, Chandler & Co and *The Vet*.

Dominic Jenkins, the heart surgeon who wanted Rob to stop smoking before he would carry out surgery, was played by **Miles Anderson**, later to act Sam Dawson in the series *Have Your Cake and Eat It*, as well as appearing in *A Touch of Frost*, *Into the Blue* and the 'Love Bites' play *In Your Dreams*.

Robert Hudson – who played PC 'Yorkie' Smith in *The Bill* for five years – acted a police inspector cautioning Will Preston's son, Tony, who found himself in trouble after striking up a friendship with Rob's son, Harry.

LANDLADY WANTS TO CALL TIME

Pub landlady Chloë White was left battling for her life when tests revealed that she was suffering from Hodgkin's disease, a form of lymphatic cancer. Devastated by the news, she tried to hide her illness from husband James, believing that he would be unable to cope. But when the problem became too big for her to deal with alone, she changed her mind.

Jack thought that the disease was in only its early stages, so he was shocked when a scan revealed that the cancer was far more advanced and had reached her abdomen. Chloë gave up and refused treatment. She saw no point in having chemotherapy if she was going to die anyway.

Beth drove the angry young mum to her own father's grave and told her of the pain she felt when he died from a heart attack in his eighties. What, she asked, would Chloë's daughter, Sarah-Jane, feel on visiting the grave of her

ABOVE LEFT
It's Jack to the rescue again when a bully's attack on Harry Clulow and Tony Preston backfires and he ends up with a severed artery in his leg.

RIGHT
Jack smells trouble when Richard Morris (Alan David) plans to build a generator powered by pig sewage.

mother, a 35-year-old woman who died without even try-ing to fight back?

This convinced Chloë to change her mind. After facing up to the gruelling treatment, Jack delivered the wonderful news that her cell count had vastly improved and her can-cer was in remission. Chloë was now able to take a break in her treatment programme while further tests were car-ried out.

PIG OF A NEIGHBOUR

• Pig farmer Richard Morris was played by **Alan David**, who acted Rovers Return relief manager Glyn Thomas in *Coronation Street*, Dick Robertshaw in *Emmerdale* and Bernie in *Making Out*, as well as appearing in the sitcoms *The Squirrels*, *Foxy Lady*, *There Comes a Time* and *Honey for Tea*.

When Jack bought himself a cottage in Cardale, he was driven round the bend by his new neighbour, Richard Morris, and his large collection of pigs. The farmer spent his days and nights banging and crashing around as he built a generator powered by pig muck. Jack sealed up his windows to keep out the gut-wrenching stink and shouted at Alberta, Richard's saucy sow, when she came calling. The GP's ordeal was dramatically relieved when the methane burner exploded with a loud bang and Richard, blackened by the blast, decided to sell his herd of pigs and start his alternative energy project again with a windmill.

• **Maurice Denham** returned to the role of Battle of Britain veteran Douglas Hart in an episode that featured a spectacular sequence with Spitfires flying over a dam at Ladybower reservoir, where the Dam Busters practised during the Second World War.

This presented a challenge to *Peak Practice* chief production buyer John Steppings. 'I was asked to get hold of two Spitfires,' he recalls. 'I found one in Cambridgeshire and the second one was at the time in Czechoslovakia.

'We flew the Spitfires to Cranwell RAF College, but we couldn't get them off the ground because it snowed for three days. Then we had a message that there was going to be a short window of opportunity.

'We sat by the reservoir for ages and, suddenly, we heard the drones of the Spitfires coming over. For about half-an-hour we had radio control with them. An RAF fighter instructor called Charlie Brown flew one of them and we had three cameras rolling to make sure we got some beautiful shots. It was a magical day, *Boy's Own* stuff, to be in charge of two Spitfires.'

Another war veteran in the story was played by **George Malpas**, who had already taken three roles in *Coronation Street* and played postman Barney in *Emmerdale*'s early days, as well as appearing in programmes such as *Our Day Out, Barchester Chronicles, Mapp and Lucia, Brookside, EastEnders* and *Kavanagh QC* (as John Thaw's father), and films such as *Indiana Jones and the Last Crusade*.

Isabel de Gines's friend Ken Alton, who drove Douglas Hart to the fly-past, was played by **Frank Windsor**, best known as detective John Watt in *Z Cars*, and for roles in *Softly Softly* and *Softly Softly: Task Force*. He also acted Harry Bradley in two series of *Flying Lady*, the title role in *The Real Eddy English* and, more recently, Cyril Wendage in *September Song*.

Dye factory boss Ken Alton accompanies Douglas Hart and Isabel de Gines to a Spitfire fly-past commemorating the Battle of Britain.

Despite suffering from two small strokes, Cardale's ex-RAF squadron leader, Douglas Hart, planned a trip to a Spitfire fly-past to commemorate the Battle of Britain, ignoring the protests of his companion, Alice North, who had moved into his home to care for him. Douglas fell out with Alice when she told Will about his lapses of memory, and she was hurt when Will gave him the go-ahead. As a result, Douglas attended the fly-past with Isabel de Gines and her friend, dye factory boss Ken Alton, instead of with her.

While Douglas stood on the causeway at

Ladybower reservoir with his RAF comrades, drinking a toast to those 'gone but not forgotten', Isabel and her friend sat canoodling in the car. After the fly-past, Douglas suffered another stroke and fell to the ground. Ken rushed the former Spitfire pilot to hospital in his car, but Douglas died there.

Alice waited at home to make up with her friend after preparing a meal and setting the table with the best china. On hearing the news, she was angry and frustrated that no one had taken her advice. Isabel consoled Alice by telling her that Douglas had himself planned to call into the farm shop on the way home to buy her favourite fruit cake as a peace offering.

THE WORKAHOLIC TYPE

Workaholic Carol Dart, a typist at Cardale Dyes, was found to have repetitive strain injury after consulting Jack about severe wrist pains. He prescribed anti-inflammatory drugs and told Carol to rest. Concerned that her boss, Ken Alton, might be forcing his employee to work long hours, Jack spoke to Beth, who was the dye works' medical officer.

Although she had inspected the factory, Beth admitted that she had overlooked the offices and promised that she would rectify this. When Carol later confessed to Jack that she had sneaked back into the office during the weekends and evenings to ensure she kept on top of her work, he was angry and confronted Beth. He later apologised and they started getting on better again.

A FATHER'S ANGER

Sue Keel, who took a job as cleaner at The Beeches, was embarrassed when milkman husband Martin – reeling from just having been sacked from his job – overreacted by rushing son Matthew to the surgery with a mild virus when the anxious father noticed he looked unwell.

As Martin cared for Matthew at home, Sue worked extra hours behind the bar at The Manor Hotel. Matthew's condition worsened and he collapsed in the garden with feverish convulsions. Terrified for his son, Martin phoned Beth, who was unable to go immediately because she was deal-

• Sue Keel, The Beeches' cleaner whose husband Martin struck Beth when he was concerned about the fate of his son, Matthew, was played by **Minnie Driver**, who acted on TV in *Mr Wroe's Virgins* and *The Politician's Wife* before taking Hollywood by storm and appearing in films such as *Sleepers*, *Grosse Pointe Blank*, *Good Will Hunting* and *Hard Rain*.

Beth is on the receiving end of Martin Keel's frustration after his long wait for her to see his son Matthew, who suffered a febrile convulsion.

- When Jack's schizophrenic first love, Karen Eastman, tracked him down to The Beeches, her father, David, was played by veteran actor **Tenniel Evans**. Since starring in the sixties legal series *The Sullavan Brothers*, his many television appearances have included character roles in *Inspector Morse, The Bill, Heartbeat* and *Hetty Wainthropp Investigates.*

ing with another patient. Becoming increasingly angry, Martin repeatedly called practice manager Kim Beardsmore and demanded that she send a doctor straight-away.

In desperation, Martin called for an ambulance. As it drove off to hospital, Beth arrived at the Keels' house. Having heard the ambulancemen saying that his son might have meningitis, Martin was panic-stricken – and furious. He lashed out at Beth, striking her across the face with such force that she was thrown into the side of her car door. Cut and bleeding, she pushed Martin in anger before getting back into her car and driving away.

Back at the hospital, Matthew was diagnosed with viral meningitis, a less serious form of the potentially fatal illness. After crying on Will's shoulder, Beth decided to report the incident with Martin to the police and have him struck off the surgery's lists. But when Jack was called to help Martin after he had deliberately cut his hand, it became apparent that the unemployed father was suffering from depression. After having his damaged tendons repaired in hospital, Martin was referred by Jack to a psychologist. As a result, Beth withdrew her statement to the police, but stuck to her decision that he should no longer be treated at The Beeches.

JACK'S BLAST FROM THE PAST

The past came back to haunt Jack when his first true love, Karen Eastman, phoned him at The Beeches. The pair had been engaged when they were medical students, but they split up when Karen became ill with schizophrenia and Jack had found the strain unbearable.

Her condition could be stabilised with drugs but relapses would occur without them. Now was such a time and, convinced that those around her were trying to poison her, Karen wanted Jack by her side in London. When a second call from a psychiatric hospital came through, Jack felt it was his duty to go to her. Trying to comfort her there, Jack was shocked when she screamed in terror at him and shouted that he was an imposter.

Later, Karen discharged herself from the hospital and hitched a lift to Cardale. Entering The Beeches, Karen sat at Jack's desk, stethoscope round her neck, convinced that

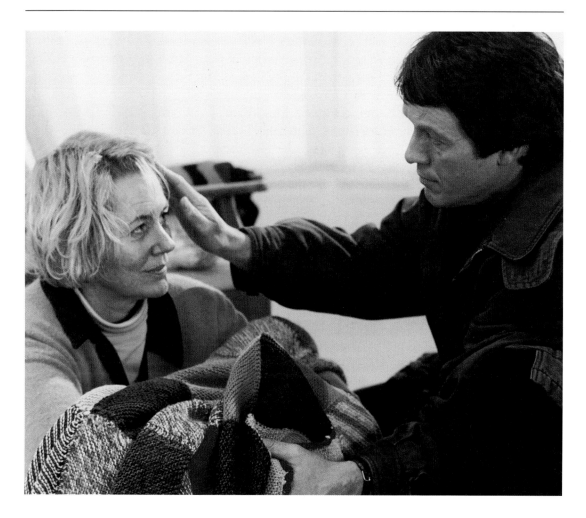

Jack's one-time fiancée Karen Eastman (Dearbhla Molloy) returns into his life unexpectedly.

she was a doctor at the practice. Alarmed that there was an intruder in the building, Beth phoned the police, but Jack turned up, realised that it was Karen and went in. Emerging moments later, Jack introduced Karen to Beth, who, though shell-shocked, showed her support by inviting both of them to stay at her house.

As Karen slept upstairs, Jack explained to Beth what had happened to Karen and confessed that he felt ashamed for often wishing her dead. Beth's efforts to be sympathetic were interrupted by a loud crash from upstairs as Karen smashed a bedroom mirror with her bare hands. The two GPs bandaged her up and the next morning Jack drove her back to the psychiatric hospital. In a moment of clarity, Karen insisted that Jack must never come to see her again, however much she pleaded with him. Jack left the hospital, released from a great burden that he had carried for years.

BETH AGAINST THE ELEMENTS

While Jack attended Cardale Football Club's victory dinner after the village team had won a coveted trophy, Beth had a secret meeting with her ex-lover, Dr Michael Cummings, at a country hotel. Arriving late, Michael wasted no time in telling Beth that he and his wife, Antonia, had separated and he wanted to rekindle their romance. Initially tempted, Beth turned him down and drove home to Jack, who was sitting on her sofa waiting to tell her that he loved her.

The night was filthy and heavy rain made driving difficult. As Beth made her way through the meandering lanes of the High Peak, she was stopped by a young man, Sean, asking for help. He had crashed his car and his girlfriend, Lisa, was trapped in the upturned vehicle at the bottom of the craggy hillside.

Unable to get a mobile phone reception and call for help in such a remote area, Beth gave Sean her car keys and told him to get assistance while she stayed to care for Lisa. As the hours dragged by, Lisa confessed that the car was stolen and Sean, whom she had met only that evening, would have been frightened of getting into trouble. He had, in fact, dumped Beth's car and gone home to bed. Giving Lisa a shot of morphine to kill her pain and wrapping her in a thick blanket, Beth set off to get help. But blizzard-like conditions meant that she had to turn back.

Back in Cardale, Jack's panic turned to anger on hearing a message from Michael on Beth's answer machine – unaware that Beth was fighting for survival in the bitter cold. As Lisa's condition deteriorated, Beth struggled back up to the roadside, where she lit a beacon, then returned to her young patient and cuddled up to Lisa to keep them both warm.

Sean's brother, Damien, concerned about the condition Sean was in, called out Will, who simply assumed that he was suffering from a hangover. On receiving a call from the local police informing him that Beth's car had been found abandoned, Will went to tell Jack, but Jack was unconcerned, still smarting from finding out about her secret assignation. When Will was called back to see Sean again, Jack accompanied him, and this time Damien's girlfriend, Susie, revealed how Sean had really sustained his injuries

• Amanda Burton had few happy memories of filming a scene where Beth became stranded on the moors in the bitter cold while trying to rescue a woman called Lisa, whose car had overturned. It was shot during the night in the middle of December.

'I don't think I've ever been so cold in my life,' she said afterwards. 'It was well below freezing and there was snow on the ground. I had to fall in a river and I had to film it three times to get it right. There was a stuntwoman there, but I decided I wanted to do the whole scene myself – it makes it more realistic. I've never had to do anything like that before.'

Stunt double **Abbi Collins**, who previously stood in for Amanda on *Boon* and has since worked with her on *Silent Witness*, was reduced to doing mostly long shots filmed by a second unit after the main action had been wrapped up.

'Amanda is a very gutsy person,' recalls Abbi. 'She did all the action herself with the first unit and I doubled everything with the second unit because there was a lot of her running across the moors in long shot, which included falling and sliding down the banking.

Beth braves the elements to help Lisa (Elizabeth Chadwick) after a car accident in a remote part of the Peaks.

'This was shot at night in the middle of winter on the moors and, if anything, Amanda was out in it more than I was. She was bitterly cold. I kept asking whether I could take over, but was told that I had to go off to do second-unit work and she just got on with it and it looked great.

'Amanda had to slip and fall into the stream, which she did. With stunts, it often isn't life-threatening, but it's horrendously uncomfortable. If the actress is supposed to be in freezing water, they will usually put in a double and do it as a long shot. But she wants to do, and is capable of doing, so much of her own stuff. She will really have a go.'

and Sean deliriously uttered Lisa's name.

The two doctors contacted the emergency services and set out to search for Beth themselves. Her burned-out beacon led them to the spot and they hurried down the hillside to the crashed car. Jack dashed over to help, but Lisa was already dead. His heart pounded furiously as he discovered the spent syringes and Beth's medical bag. As he turned back into the snow, Jack saw her lying semi-conscious next to a tree stump. He dashed to Beth's side and, as he cradled her in his arms, she asked him to marry her.

ANGIE'S LAST DANCE

When tests revealed that dancer Angie Wilkes was suffering from the brittle-bone disease osteoporosis, the talented performer was devastated, despite her friend Beth's assurances that her condition could be treated with hormone-replacement therapy. Dancing was Angie's life – she taught it and was currently working with her star pupil, Ben, who was putting a lot of energy into an audition piece.

Beth ordered Angie to rest from dancing, but she dosed herself up with painkillers and made her way to the dance studio to put Ben through his paces, before dancing alone in her private world.

She returned home, resigned to the fact that she would probably never dance properly again. That evening her university lecturer husband, Drew, came home from work to find her collapsed on the floor with a stomach bleed caused by the painkillers. Following a brief spell in hospital, Angie confided in Drew about the osteoporosis. The two decided to face it together and announced to their friends that they would be moving to Drew's native South Africa to make a fresh start.

• Top choreographer **Arlene Phillips**, best known for her work with the raunchy dance troupe Hot Gossip, was responsible for sequences in the episode featuring Beth's dancer friend Angie Wilkes, whose career was shattered by the brittle-bone disease osteoporosis.

Angie Wilkes (Donna King) faces up to a future without dancing after being diagnosed with osteoporosis.

FUNDHOLDING ARRIVES

Immersing himself in The Beeches to forget his failing marriage, Will had taken on the mountain of work necessary to make it a fundholding practice with control of its own budgets. He was helped in his task by practice manager Kim Beardsmore, with whom he built up a close friendship. She also provided an understanding ear into which he could pour both his marital problems and the opposition to fundholding from Beth. The senior partner even stormed out of a meeting held to discuss the controversial move, although Kim's diplomacy later persuaded her to go along with it.

However, Will felt slightly awkward when Kim called at his house with an Indian takeaway and a bottle of wine. After the pair attempted a tipsy kiss, Kim asked if she could be considered for the position of fund manager. Knowing that she did not have the experience necessary, Will had to turn her down, but insisted that, as The Beeches continued to grow, so would Kim's salary as practice manager.

Will and Jack surprised even themselves when they were so impressed with bank manager Trevor Sharp at his interview that they appointed him to the new post.

Dr Stuart Mosely (Jonathan Hyde) shocks Will with the news that he is HIV-positive.

A FRIEND IN NEED

Will was devastated when his close friend Dr Stuart Mosely, best man at his wedding to Sarah, turned up at The Beeches with the news that he was HIV positive and showing the first signs of full-blown AIDS. Stuart, who had left a glittering career as a GP for an executive position with a charity, also had retinitis – an inflammation of the retina – which would eventually leave him blind.

Wanting to keep his condition a secret to protect his family – and not jeopardise a place at medical school for his daughter Sally, who wanted to become a doctor – he asked Will to treat him at home. The GP agreed but implored his friend, in vain, to contact the health authorities where he had treated patients while being knowingly infected.

Will insisted that he would consult the Director of Public Health for advice, but would wait for a while to give Stuart the chance to talk to his family and friends. His wife, Zoë, also wanted secrecy and begged Will to lie to Stuart that his death certificate would not reveal he had died from AIDS.

On being asked to supply Stuart with enough drugs for an overdose, the doctor passed him into Jack's care. Stuart went ahead with his suicide plan, using tablets from his bathroom cabinet, but it was thwarted by Will calling round to see him.

When it emerged that Stuart contracted the disease from his gay lover, Alan, who had died from AIDS two years earlier, daughter Sally hugged her father and promised that she would protect her mother from the truth. She supported her father's wishes to die before AIDS took hold and supplied him with enough tablets to take a fatal overdose.

CARAVAN FAMILY MOVE

The Clarke family – 'Clarkey', Lou and their two young children – lived in a cold, damp caravan parked in the middle of a muddy farmyard miles away from anywhere. Heavily pregnant, Lou had found it difficult to attend the local antenatal clinic and refused a home visit from the midwife because she was ashamed of the family's squalid living conditions.

At a routine check-up with Beth at The Beeches, Lou was found to be suffering from high blood pressure, possibly caused by overwork. She was admitted to hospital as a precaution against pre-eclampsia – a toxic condition of pregnancy – and Beth drove round to give 'Clarkey' the news. On discovering the family's appalling living conditions, Beth persuaded Jack – who had moved in with her – to let his empty cottage to them, as they had nowhere else to go.

SARAH LEAVES WILL

Will had done everything in his power to save his crumbling marriage. He and wife Sarah tackled their financial problems by moving to a smaller house in a less salubrious area and Sarah took a part-time job as secretary at the village school to boost family funds.

But Sarah soon became bored with her job and was offered another by drugs rep Peter Doland, who flirted outrageously with her over a drink. When Will arrived home,

• When the Clarke family were seen in Cardale, it proved to be a family affair on and off screen. Actor Richard Platt, who plays The Manor Hotel landlord James White, welcomed his real-life partner, **Tracy Brabin**, on set as Lou Clarke. She later played Tricia Armstrong in *Coronation Street*, which **Ian Mercer** – who played her husband, 'Clarkey', in *Peak Practice* – also joined, as Gary Mallett.

Tracy played Sandra in two series of *A Bit of a Do* and Ginny in three series of *Outside Edge*. Ian acted policemen in *Cracker* and *A Touch of Frost*, as well as Guy Simmons in the first series of *Common as Muck*.

Gaynor Faye, later to play Gary Mallett's wife, Judy, in *Coronation Street*, appeared in two episodes of *Peak Practice* as WPC Benson. Gaynor, daughter of screenwriter Kay Mellor, also acted in *Downwardly Mobile*, *Medics*, *Men of the World* and her mother's drama *Some Kind of Life*.

he was startled to find Sarah celebrating her new job with a bottle of champagne. Peter later phoned to say that he was sorry, but he had spoken prematurely and there was no job after all.

Sarah had deliberately kept Will in the dark about Peter because she knew how much her husband disliked the man. Will told Sarah that he was fed up of her 'tedious tantrums' and added, 'If you don't begin to make an investment in the family, then that's it, the end.' Sarah continued to stir up bad feeling and Will became cold towards her. Facing up to the fact that their marriage was over, Sarah moved into a flat, taking sons Tony and Julian with her. Will now had to adjust to living on his own with weekend visits from his children.

RUNAWAY TURNS UP IN CARDALE

When a teenaged girl living rough arrived in Cardale at the same time as a baby was found dead on Stanton Moor, many assumed that she was its mother. With only the clothes that she stood up in, Abbey begged in shop doorways, stole milk and broke into the church when she needed somewhere to sleep.

She also hurled abuse at Steve behind the counter in the fish-and-chip shop after he refused to give her a portion of sausage and chips when she was 10p short. Later that evening, he found Abbey squatting in an alleyway as she injected her thigh and, mistaking her for a drug addict, destroyed the girl's syringes and punched her in the stomach.

Pensioner Alice North, who had earlier given her money, took pity on Abbey after finding the teenager sleeping in her hen house. At The Beeches, Abbey demanded to see a doctor but refused to complete a registration card and ran out before Jack had had a chance to give her a proper consultation. She tried to steal chocolate bars from the village grocer's and made a run for it, with the shopkeeper in hot pursuit. As he tried to grab her, Abbey became hysterical, lashing out at Chloë White, who had stepped in to help her. Coming to the rescue, Jack and pub landlord James White bundled her into the back of the GP's car.

Back at The Beeches, after Abbey was cleaned up and she had calmed down, she told Jack that she had diabetes. He

• Down-and-out Abbey, a runaway from a children's home, was played by *Samantha Morton* before she went on to find fame as teenage prostitute Tracy Richards in *Band of Gold*. Samantha herself grew up in children's homes before finding a career in acting, working in programmes such as *Soldier Soldier* and *Cracker*.

She has since appeared on TV as Harriet Smith in *Jane Austen's Emma*, the title role in *Jane Eyre* and Sophia Western in *The History of Tom Jones: A Foundling*, as well as starring in the films *Under the Skin* and *This is the Sea*.

The role of Inspector Rossiter, who discovered

Abbey's true identity, was played by **Eamon Boland**, who is often cast as policemen. He also acted Clive in *Singles*, Gerry Hollis in *Kinsey* and Arthur Bryant in *Law and Disorder*, and has since been seen as Graham Keegan in the parliamentary serial *Annie's Bar*.

George Little, who took the role of Alan Murdoch in the same episode, had acted the Rev. Edward Ruskin in *Emmerdale*'s early years.

Abbey (Samantha Morton) is suspected of being the mother of the baby dumped in Cardale.

warned her that she would have to start eating properly because she had nearly been in a coma. He also wanted her to see an eye specialist, fearing that her sight had been damaged. After treating the girl to a meal at a nearby Little Chef, Jack and Beth took her home. An eye surgeon insisted that, without surgery, Abbey would lose her sight. With The Beeches' new fundholding status, Will was able to arrange for the operation to be done quickly at the Belvedere Clinic.

Jack's belief that Abbey was not the dead baby's mother was confirmed when Inspector Rossiter from the local police called round to inform him that the baby's mother, a 40-year-old married woman with six children, had been found. He also revealed Abbey's real identity. Her name was Pauline Jones, a 15-year-old, who had run away from a Manchester children's home two months earlier. But, before Jack had the chance to confront her, Abbey was back on the road, with Beth's stolen cheque book in her bag.

Jack eventually found her hanging out with a gang of other homeless teenagers in some derelict railway sheds, but she refused to return to the children's home. Once she had undergone surgery, Abbey was back out on the road again.

A DISTURBED MOTHER

With their wedding looming, Beth took Jack to meet her rich friends Dominic and Annie Kent, but he found the visit disturbing. He thought it odd that Annie – who was two months pregnant – had very little contact with the couple's two-year-old daughter, Victoria, who was cared for by a full-time nanny.

It emerged that Annie, who had experienced a difficult birth, did not love their daughter and did not want this next baby. Annie was told by Dr John Reginald at his private clinic at the health centre that he would not arrange an abortion until he had spoken to both her and Dominic at home.

In a desperate and highly emotional state, she drove deep into the countryside while Dominic grew increasingly worried at home. Hours later, after Dominic had called Beth round to the house, Annie walked in, cold and wet, and played a cruel trick on her husband by telling him that she had left the car in a ford with Victoria still inside. While the desperate father raced to rescue his daughter, Annie tucked Victoria up in her bed.

Afterwards, she told Dominic that she had deceived him to make him experience the fear and terror she felt all the time. Despite her husband's warning that their marriage would be finished if she went ahead with an abortion, Annie consulted Jack at The Beeches and convinced him to agree to a termination. She moved out of the family home and faced the abortion alone.

But Dominic still loved Annie and, knowing how frightened she was of hospitals, went to find her. As she was wheeled into theatre, Dominic was by Annie's side. They had both missed each other and planned to rebuild their lives after the abortion.

JACK AND BETH MARRY AT LAST

Putting their past fears behind them, Jack and Beth married in Cardale on a fine, sunny day. Beth had been worried about losing her independence, but she admitted to Jack that she had been selfish, wanting a relationship on her terms, with all the fun but none of the commitment.

It had taken her night stranded in the bitter cold of the High Peak for Beth to realise it was time to stop the sexual sparring between herself and Jack and to marry him. And marry they did, at Cardale's parish church, with Will as best man and all their friends and villagers packing the pews to share in the couple's happiness.

Jack and Beth's happiest day is watched by best man Will and Beth's closest friend, Isabel de Gines (Sylvia Syms).

A FAMILY AT WAR

Housewife Sheila Massey was bored of being stuck at home after raising son Michael, now 28, who held a managerial position within husband Bob's successful textile factory. She felt that she knew the business so well that she should be allowed a greater involvement in the running of it.

When 56-year-old Bob suffered a heart attack and was admitted to hospital after disturbing a gang of burglars stealing garden ornaments from his home, Sheila eagerly took the reins at the factory. She immediately locked horns with her son by ignoring his views and making radical decisions about overtime shifts. And she would not listen when Michael and the factory foreman, John, complained that company electrician Joe Wilson knew nothing about computers. Sheila and Bob had remained loyal to Joe, who had been with them from the business's early days.

When Bob heard of the friction at the factory, he discharged himself from hospital and arrived at work in his pyjamas. Beth rushed round to warn of the risk of Bob having another heart attack, so Michael and Sheila asked Bob to define their roles. When the squabbling continued, Bob returned to work, assuring Beth that he would take things easy. He was soon back in hospital following a more severe heart attack. As the ambulance raced him to the hospital, he stopped breathing, and both Sheila and Michael were terrified that Bob would die this time. But he was a born fighter and pulled through. Bob announced that he planned to take life easier, and mother and son made their peace and took equal responsiblity for running the factory.

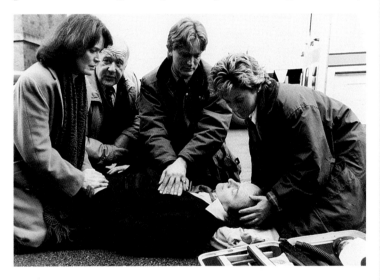

Will and Beth tend heart-attack victim Bob Massey (Tony Doyle) as wife Sheila (Judy Loe) and factory electrician Joe Wilson (Roy Barraclough) look on.

THREE DOCTORS CONNED

Beth, Jack and Will all fell foul of insurance fraudster Frank Hooley, aka Paul Carter and many other aliases, when he consulted them at The Beeches with dislocated shoulders. First, Jack signed the conman off work for a week but, as soon as he was out of the surgery, Hooley clicked his shoulder back into place, then went back to his work as an odd-

- Textile factory boss Bob Massey, who suffered a heart attack, was played by **Tony Doyle**, best known as Chief Supt John Deakin in *Between the Lines*, George Ferguson in *Band of Gold* and Brian Quigley in *Ballykissangel*.

Judy Loe, who acted Bob's wife, Sheila, appeared as Pam in the sitcom *Singles* and has also starred in *Yesterday's Dreams*, *The Chief* and *Revelations*. Sheila's son, Michael, was played by **Valentine Pelka**, brother of actress Kazia Pelka, who acts nurse Maggie Bolton in *Heartbeat*. Valentine has also taken the roles of Richard Boterel in *Cadfael* and Maurice de Bracy in *Ivanhoe*.

Roy Barraclough (above), best known as pub landlord Alec Gilroy in *Coronation Street*, played factory electrician Joe Wilson. Before returning to the *Street*, he also starred as Leslie Flitcroft in the sitcom *Mother's Ruin*.

job-man, building a dry-stone wall for Isabel de Gines.

Will did the honours when Hooley returned with his other shoulder dislocated. Days later, he was making an appointment to see Beth. When an insurance inspector called at the surgery, he explained that Hooley had worked as a contortionist and moved around the country making false claims with different insurance companies.

ALICE'S PRISON CELL ORDEAL

The long arm of the law came calling for Alice North when the old lady failed to pay her council tax. Ignoring WPC Benson's plea to pay up, she found herself in Derby's Magistrates' Court before presiding JP Isabel de Gines. Declaring knowledge of the defendant, a horrified Isabel stepped down and telephoned Beth to tell her of the OAP's confused state.

Beth arrived to check over Alice, who was then returned home. Keeping an eye on the old lady and her peculiar behaviour – talking through her letterbox to the milkman and sending a neighbour to collect her pension – Beth realised that Alice's financial problems were caused by agoraphobia, a dread of open spaces, which had developed after the death of her companion, Douglas Hart. Beth set her on the road to recovery with a prescription for mild antidepressants – and lots of visitors.

ADDICT BREAKS AND ENTERS

Trouble loomed for the Clarke family, who rented Jack's cottage, when Clarkey's younger brother, Carl – a drug user who drank heavily when he could not get a fix –

turned up to stay. On police bail for breaking and entering, the troubled teenager deceitfully obtained tranquillisers from Jack. He even asked his two young nieces where medication was kept in the house, before a twinge of conscience made him apologise.

The promise of quarry work from his brother did not stop Carl from breaking into The Manor Hotel cellar, where he was found drunk the following morning by James White. Days later, he broke into The Beeches and stole drugs from the pharmacy. After burglar alarms rang and Carl, who had injected a cocktail of drugs from his haul, gave police the slip, Isabel de Gines stumbled across him while out walking her dog and called for the police and Jack.

Recognising Isabel as a magistrate from his recent court appearance, Carl threatened both her and Jack with a kitchen knife, but backed down after they refused to be intimidated by him. He was arrested and Jack promised to find him a place in a drug rehabilitation centre. However, despite Jack explaining this to the court, the presiding magistrate was unsympathetic and sentenced Carl to a month in jail. Moved by this, Isabel resigned from the bench.

Jack is on the scene after drug user Carl Clarke (David Kitchener) is found drunk in The Manor Hotel cellar.

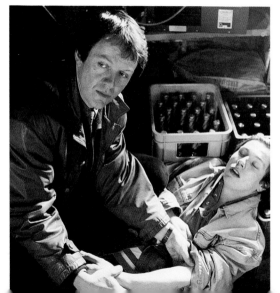

SYLVIA SYMS
as Isabel de Gines

JACQUELINE
LEONARD
as Sarah Preston

After becoming a star of the British cinema in fifties and sixties films such as *Ice Cold in Alex*, *Victim*, *East of Sudan* and *Hostile Witness*, Sylvia Sims starred as Leslie Crowther's wife in the long-running seventies television sitcom *My Good Woman*. She found one of her most compelling roles in the nineties as Beth Glover's close friend and confidante, Isabel de Gines, in *Peak Practice*.

'I liked the idea of being an older woman who is Beth's friend,' says Sylvia. 'A friendship between two women of different ages happens in real life, but it is not often explored on television.'

Beth was encouraged by magistrate Isabel in her relationship with Jack Kerruish, and was devastated when her lifelong friend died of cancer. Sylvia bowed out early in the third series of *Peak Practice* and has since been seen in many roles on television.

One role that she has played twice during her career – before and after acting Isabel – is that of former Prime Minister Lady Thatcher, first in *Thatcher: The Final Days* and then in the 'Screen Two' drama *Half the Picture*. Talking of the Iron Lady, Sylvia says, 'I can be just as formidable and ferocious as her, and often am.'

Divorced from businessman Alan Edney in 1989 after 33 years of marriage, Sylvia has a daughter, actress Beatie Edney, and a son, restaurateur Ben.

Playing Dr Will Preston's bitchy wife, Sarah, was a launching pad for actress Jacqueline Leonard. After acting in *Peak Practice* for three years and appearing briefly in the fourth series, she found a whole new audience when she joined *EastEnders* as Lorraine Wicks, David's ex-wife.

Surprisingly, acting was never an ambition for the milkman's daughter from Blackpool when she was growing up. 'Showbusiness just wasn't something that was in our family's background,' she explains. 'I went to art college and thought that I would have a career in graphics or fashion.'

Packing in art college and switching to drama school after a boyfriend started training as an actor, Jacqueline was set on the road to stardom. 'It was the best thing I could have done because it helped get rid of my shyness,' she says.

After acting with the Royal Shakespeare Company, she appeared on television in the award-winning *Memento Mori*, *A Time to Dance* and *Inspector Morse*. She also played a Yankee Doodle Dancer in director Richard Attenborough's film *Chaplin*, before landing her role in *Peak Practice*.

In real life, Jacqueline lives with actor Graham Turner, who appeared in an episode of *Peak Practice* as a victim of husband beating before starring in Lucy Gannon's prison series *Insiders*.

RICHARD PLATT
and HAZEL ELLERBY
as James and Chloë White

Playing landlord and landlady of The Manor Hotel in Cardale required no original research by Richard Platt and Hazel Ellerby, who have played James and Chloë White in *Peak Practice* since the programme began.

Richard once ran a pub in Cheshire with an ex-girlfriend's stepfather, then worked in London as a relief manager for Whitbread's brewery, and Hazel has experience as a barmaid.

Joining *Peak Practice* was also a life-changing move for Hazel, who met her husband, sound recordist Dave Sansom, while making the programme. 'We saw each other across a crowded set and fell immediately in love,' she says. 'We married in 1995 and have a baby daughter called Millie. I also have a young daughter, Sophie, by a previous relationship.'

When he began work on the series, Richard already shared his life with actress Tracy Brabin, who guest-starred in *Peak Practice* as Lou Clarke during the second series before becoming best known as single mum Tricia Armstrong in *Coronation Street*. The couple's first daughter, Lois, was born the day after Richard filmed his screen daughter Sarah-Jane's birth in *Peak Practice*. The couple have since had a second daughter, Nancy.

Before joining *Peak Practice*, the actress had 'great fun' playing Timothy Spall's wife in *Frank Stubbs Promotes*, as well as appearing in programmes such as *To Have and To Hold*, *The Bill*, *Moon and Son*, *Hale & Pace* and *Between the Lines*. Most of Richard's previous experience was on stage, including work with Peter Hall's National Theatre company. He also directed his own short picture, *Mayday, Mayday*, which featured on- and off-screen partners Hazel and Tracy and won an award from the First Film Foundation.

SHELAGH McLEOD
as Dr Kate Webster

Shelagh McLeod's arrival as Dr Kate Webster at the Brompton Health Centre in Cardale in 1996 brought new meaning to Will Preston's life following his divorce.

Canadian-born Shelagh, who began her acting career in Britain, once had a holiday job as an ancillary nurse at a hospital to help her through drama school. A few years ago, the actress – who in her early teens was diagnosed as having degenerative scoliosis, a hunchback condition – underwent two gruelling operations to realign her spine and then spent five days in intensive care when her lung failed to reinflate. Shelagh and her second husband, property developer Marek Pilkington Miksa, have one daughter, Katherine.

1995

The third series of *Peak Practice* proved to be the final one starring Kevin Whately and Amanda Burton. Simon Shepherd also talked about leaving at the end of the series, because he saw nowhere left for the character of Dr Will Preston to go. 'All the stars kept changing their minds about who was going to leave,' reveals Michele Buck, who took over as producer from Tony Virgo after working on programmes such as *Crossroads* and *Boon*. In the event, when Kevin and Amanda confirmed their departure, following newspaper allegations of an affair between them, Simon had good reason to stay, because Will would take charge of The Beeches.

On screen, life went on as normal in the 1995 series. Set a year after Jack and Beth's wedding, it began dramatically with a cave rescue and went on to cover issues such as husband beating, alcoholism, cancer, psychiatric care in the community and Alzheimer's disease.

Another drama during the 15-episode marathon came for Jack when a car crash caused a pregnant woman to go into premature labour and he had to deliver the baby at the roadside. When the baby was discovered to be brain damaged, the family complained of negligence on Jack's part. After the case was dropped, a disillusioned Jack returned to Zimbabwe for two months to help in setting up a new clinic, leaving Beth fearing that he might leave her and his problems at The Beeches for ever. Drama of a different kind came for Will and wife Sarah, who finally decided to divorce, but Will found new love briefly with drugs company representative Janey Cooper.

A new face in the regular cast as practice nurse Laura Elliott – who replaced Ellie Ndebala following the departure of actress Sharon Hinds – was Veronica Roberts, previously seen in *Sam*, *Tenko*, *The Bill*, *EastEnders*, *Harry* and *Casualty*, as well as on the West End stage in *Miss Julie* and *Dancing at Lughnasa*. Another actress to leave during the series broadcast in 1995 was Sylvia Syms, when her character, Isabel de Gines, died from cancer. But the arrival of Gary Mavers as trainee GP Andrew Attwood in Episode 10 gave the programme the first of its new generation of doctors who would be seen over the next three series.

'We always knew, while making the third series, that there was a chance that either Kevin Whately or Simon Shepherd would leave,' says then producer Michele Buck. 'So we invented a trainee GP who could have filled either role. Will was posh and Jack was more working-class, but Andrew was younger and trendier, and in one respect filled Simon's role but in another filled Jack's with his working-class background.'

Off screen, Central Television, which produced the programme, was now owned by Carlton. Tony Virgo departed to set up his own production company and make two series of *The Vet* for the BBC, and creator Lucy Gannon ended her association with the programme, deciding to concentrate on other projects after two series. As a result, an eight-strong team of writers was used on this run of *Peak Practice*.

One story they did not come up with was an affair for Jack or Beth. 'If I had stayed on,' reveals Lucy, 'I think I would have had one of them being unfaithful, falling in love passionately with someone else.' Instead, Lucy left and created another winning ITV series, *Bramwell*, about a headstrong female doctor running a small hospital in Victorian England. She was also to write the one-off drama *Trip Trap*, in which Kevin Whately shook off his genial screen image by playing a violent husband.

The ITV Network Centre explored the idea of turning *Peak Practice* into a soap opera in half-hour episodes, but it came to nothing. 'They thought they had something very successful that they could strip down and make run for ever,' says Michele Buck. 'But *Peak Practice* doesn't strip down very easily. Although you have mythical Cardale, it's all shot outside. The doctors are rarely in the surgery – they're in lots of locations. To keep it as *Peak Practice*, but increase the output, would have been too expensive. I think the thought of making it a soap was also one of the things that made Kevin and Amanda leave.'

FOLLOWING PAGE *Gary Mavers joined Kevin Whately, Simon Shepherd and Amanda Burton two-thirds of the way through the 1995 series as Andrew Attwood, when producer Michele Buck believed that one of her two male stars would leave at the end of filming.*

THE CHARACTERS

DR JACK KERRUISH (Kevin Whately)
Married to Beth for a year, Jack has finally shown himself willing to commit himself to a relationship. He is also dedicated to his patients, determined to give them the best care possible. But a complaint of negligence threatens his job and marriage.

DR BETH GLOVER (Amanda Burton)
Although she has accepted fundholding status for The Beeches, Beth still hates talking about money and patients in the same breath. Her priority is providing quality care for all of her patients. She is very happy with married life.

DR WILL PRESTON (Simon Shepherd)
Following the break-up of his marriage to Sarah, Will has emerged a much stronger person. Missing his two sons, he throws himself into his work and finds happiness with a drugs company representative.

**DR ANDREW ATTWOOD
(Gary Mavers)**
Dr Andrew Attwood arrives at The Beeches from Liverpool as a trainee GP. After working as an electrician at a car factory, he started training as a doctor, inspired to do so by the work-related lung disease that caused his father's death.

SARAH PRESTON (Jacqueline Leonard)
A tragic accident involving son Tony looks set to reunite Sarah with ex-husband Will, but he has to choose between his head and his heart.

ISABEL DE GINES (Sylvia Syms)
Beth's trusted friend Isabel, who has lived a life of great energy and vitality, has to face up to the news that she is suffering from pancreatic cancer and has not long to live.

KIM BEARDSMORE (Esther Coles)
Practice manager Kim continues to look for love after her close work with Will in setting up The Beeches as a fundholding practice never quite led to the romance for which she had hoped.

LAURA ELLIOTT (Veronica Roberts)
Vivacious new practice nurse Laura is a divorcée who left her womanising and alcoholic doctor husband after ten years of marriage when her son – now grown up – was only seven.

**JAMES and CHLOE WHITE
(Richard Platt and Hazel Ellerby)**
The Manor Hotel landlord James is relieved that wife Chloë has been given the all-clear following a course of chemotherapy for Hodgkin's disease, a form of lymphatic cancer.

ALICE NORTH (Margery Mason)
Pensioner Alice has been cured of her agoraphobia, which came on after the death of her companion, Douglas Hart, and can face the outside world again.

TREVOR SHARP (Shaun Prendergast)
Appointed as fund manager at The Beeches, former bank manager Trevor keeps a close eye on the practice's spending and is now married to Leanda.

LEANDA SHARP (Beth Goddard)
Hairdresser Leanda is now married to her long-time boyfriend Trevor, who found a new job at The Beeches.

- Actor **Tim Dutton** was rushed to hospital after knocking himself out while filming his role as Alan 'Tommo' Tomlins, leader of the cave rescue team that Jack joined when a group of schoolchildren became stranded.

'We were working in an underground cave, which was quite dark and narrow, and I just walked into a rock and bashed my head,' said 6ft 3in-tall Tim, who previously played Donna Tucker's lover in *Soldier Soldier*. 'I tried to carry on but felt very dizzy and lost my memory, so the medical adviser, Debra Grimley, insisted on getting me to hospital.

'I had X-rays and found out I had whiplash and delayed concussion, so I was very relieved she'd been so professional and sorted me out so quickly. I had to have a couple of days off work but, luckily, when I got back most of my scenes were lying down!'

The episode was filmed at Bagshaw Cavern and caves at the Heights of Abraham with the assistance of Derbyshire Cave Rescue.

Teacher Caroline Royal, who suffered a broken leg in the story, was played by **Siobhan Finneran**, previously seen as Josie Phillips in *Coronation Street* and subsequently as Heather Hutchinson in *Emmerdale*.

Meryl Hampton took the role of Marie McKenner, one of the student's mothers, seven years after she was last seen in *Crossroads* as Margaret Grice, wife of layabout Ray.

Debra Grimley became a medical adviser to *Peak Practice* at the start of the third series, after working as a practice nurse manager in a Nottingham GP's surgery. It was her job to demonstrate to the actors how doctors give injections, take blood pressure and temperatures, and any other techniques needed.

'There are lots of people watching the series who have medical knowledge, because of their jobs or because they have been patients themselves,' says Debra. 'It's my job to make sure all the medical details are as accurate as possible.'

She also had to provide medical cover on set and was on hand when Amanda Burton gashed her lip badly during Beth's dramatic rescue of farmer Tim Shardlow after his attempted suicide. 'Amanda had to wrench the door of a car open quickly,' recalls Debra. 'Unfortunately, the door hit her in the mouth and lacerated her lip. Her lip swelled up quite badly but, after I treated her with ice packs, Amanda got straight back into filming.'

Tim Shardlow was played by prolific character actor **Paul Copley**, whose television roles have included Ian in *Roughnecks*, Jerry in the cult BBC2 series *This Life* and Peter Quinlan in writer Jimmy McGovern's *The Lakes*.

BETH FEARS FOR JACK'S SAFETY

Beth and Jack spent their first wedding anniversary apart, with Jack out on a cave rescue. At first, Beth thought that Jack had forgotten their special date, but her annoyance turned to fears for his safety when she discovered that Jack's services as a medic were needed by a cave rescue team. They had been called out to save a group of A-level geography students trapped by a landfall at a disused lead mine and were in grave danger of being drowned by flooding in the mine shafts.

RIGHT *Jack joins a cave rescue team and ends up examining one of his colleagues, Alan 'Tommo' Tomlins (Tim Dutton), after a landfall crushes his chest.*

Alan 'Tommo' Tomlins, one of the most experienced members of the rescue team, decided the quickest way to reach the students was through The Devil's Throat, a terrifying network of caves and siphons about a mile away that would lead them to the mine shafts.

As Tommo, Jack and some others began their climb through the earth's belly – leaving rescue co-ordinator Cleary with a team of volunteers digging through the rock fall – the dark, wet and confined conditions made Jack claustrophobic, but he carried on, determined not to crack up. Conditions worsened when they had to struggle through a passage flooded by heavy rain.

Marie McKenner, the mother of student Alison, who was trapped below, had earlier that day stormed out of The Beeches after Beth refused to give her some tranquillisers for stress. Now, she waited on the surface with her GP, both of them desperately worried for those below. Underground, Jack panicked when his lantern went out after being left alone for a while in a pitch-black, water-filled siphon. 'I've got to get out,' he screamed. As Tommo came to his aid, Jack pulled himself together.

The team finally bumped into Alison, who had left the rest of the party to seek help. When she led them to the other students, Jack found them in shock and their teacher, Caroline Royal, suffering from a broken leg. As Jack stayed with his patients, Tommo's attempt to dig a way out caused a sec-ond landfall, which crushed his chest, causing a collapsed lung and internal bleeding. Jack punched a tube into his side to make his breathing easier and helped the others to strap him on to a stretcher.

The wounded were then carried to safety through a small entrance in the rocks. Anxious bystanders hugged their loved ones and Jack momentarily left Tommo – with whom he had formed a close reliatiship – to embrace Beth. When he rejoined Tommo, Jack was heartbroken to find that he had died.

NEW FACES AT THE BEECHES

The Beeches, now a fully fledged fundholding practice, continued to go from strength to strength, with former bank manager Trevor Sharp taking up his appointment as fund manager. The arrival of a new nurse, Laura Elliott, saw a no-nonsense approach and forthright manner that had many of the awkward and cantankerous old patients like putty in her hands.

Trevor occasionally ruffled feathers by pointing out the financial implications of the doctors' actions. But he sailed a little too close to the wind when he ticked Beth off for using up the fund for infertility treatments. She insisted that she would not allow Trevor to dictate medical ethics.

PLAYING WITH FIRE

When experienced firefighter George Milton suffered from blurred vision, blackouts and nausea, he was desperate to keep his troubles from Chief Officer Gilzean. But Beth dis-covered that George was having problems with his hearing when she was instructed to carry out medical examinations on all the fire staff. She recommended that he have further tests, but he persuaded Beth not to say anything until the exact problem was known.

At the christening party for George's granddaughter, Jack and Beth found George collapsed on the floor, uncon-scious. Beth helped him to his feet and promised not to say anything there and then on condition that he visited her at

• Vertigo-suffering fireman George Milton was played by **Freddie Fletcher**, who as Merchant Navy seaman Bob Whitely had enjoyed an affair with Bet Lynch in *Coronation Street*, as well as appearing in *Emmerdale* as crook Derek Warner. Years earlier, he had acted *Street* actress Lynne Perrie's son in director Ken Loach's acclaimed film *Kes*. In *Peak Practice*, his wife, Pam, was played by former *Play School* and *Play Away* presen-ter **Carol Leade**.

The Beeches the next morning. When George failed to turn up, Beth spoke to his wife, Pam, who was unaware of her husband's illness.

Later that day, when a 15-year-old epileptic boy became trapped on the ledge of a tall derelict building, Beth discovered that George had been despatched to retrieve the teenager. Unable to handle the responsibility of ending George's career by telling his boss, she went up in the crane lift with him instead to rescue the boy.

When George admitted to suffering from vertigo, Beth concluded that he was suffering from Ménière's disease, a disorder of the inner ear that would eventually leave him deaf. George could no longer continue with his fireman's duties and, facing up to his problems, he decided to take a desk job within the service.

Beth takes drastic action when she discovers that fireman George Milton (Freddie Fletcher) suffers from blackouts and vertigo.

• **Tom Chadbon** acted Alice North's landlord, Patrick Hargreave, after playing many character roles on television. He has since been seen as Senior Crown Prosecutor Lenny Monk in the series *Crown Prosecutor* and Frank Crawley in the mini-series *Rebecca*.

In the same episode, Father Kelly was played by *Ron Davies*, best known as Ivy Tilsley's fiancé George Wardle in *Coronation Street* before she dumped him on finding out that he was a divorcé.

WILL'S POLITICAL AMBITIONS

Will put paid to his plans to become a Conservative councillor when he found out that the man responsible for nominating him – local property developer Patrick Hargreave – was also the landlord of pensioner Alice North, who had been poisoned when an archaic water heater emitted toxic gas.

Believing Hargreave to be responsible, Will decided that he could not be party to Hargreave's nomination and completely blew his chances of election at the selection interview. He then took Hargreave to task over Alice, but his indignation turned to embarrassment when the old lady later told him that she had turned down her landlord's offer of central heating.

COMMUNITY'S LACK OF CARE

• Former psychiatric patient Cissy Banks was played by **Petra Markham**, who had in the seventies acted Lydia Hackett in the comedy series *Albert and Victoria* and has more recently played Grace Forster in *Plotlands*.

Care in the community came to Cardale when four former psychiatric patients, Cissy, Muriel, Freddie and Terry, moved into a 'group home' in the village. Cardale folk wanted the home closed down, and its residents were blamed when seven-year-old Eddie Harding, who lived next door, became seriously ill with Weill's disease, an illness spread by rats.

Eddie's father, Martin, organised a protest meeting for villagers to attend. When Terry was taken ill at the home, Jack feared that Martin might be right and arranged for a visit from pest control in the hope that the source of the disease could be found. To Jack's relief, the group home was given a clean bill of health and Terry was found to be suffering from gallstones.

When the two other young Harding children told Jack of a nearby pond and stream where they had recently been fishing and swimming, the GP decided to investigate and found the rat-infested carcass of a sheep lying by the waterside. When Jack took his findings to Martin's meeting, villagers did not seem interested – they just wanted the home closed. But Jack appealed to their better natures and told them that the residents belonged in Cardale, not shut up in an institution.

Meanwhile, at the group home, romance blossomed for Muriel and Freddie, who became engaged. Freddie, an elderly virgin, accepted Muriel's proposal of marriage, but only after a lesson on the birds and the bees from Jack.

• Stepping into the role of Rebecca Dawson, who was suffering from an infected tattoo, was **Judy Brooke**, who had previously experienced even greater tragedy on television by dying of a drugs overdose in *Children's Ward* and from hepatitis B in *Medics*.

'It started to become a bit of a running joke,' recalls Judy. 'Every part I went for, there was something wrong with me. But I was glad to know I didn't die in *Peak Practice*, although in the story they thought I might because rats were on the loose in the village and I was showing symptoms of Weill's disease.'

Rebecca had a small, Celtic-designed tattoo on her

REBECCA'S SECRET TATTOO

After losing her husband to cancer a year earlier, Cath Dawson had become overprotective towards her daughter, Rebecca, smothering her in the process. Rebecca, who worked in the mobile library but longed to study at art college, felt it would be too hard on her mother if she went away, and gave up her dreams of an art qualification. In the meantime, she secretly nursed an infected tattoo on her back, of which she knew her mother would disapprove.

Cath called Will to their home when she noticed that Rebecca was in pain. On discovering her tattoo, Will

left arm, but the infection was caused by a massive Trojan horse design on her back. 'I was in make-up for almost three hours having it put on,' says Judy. 'That was only used for one day's filming, but the one on my arm had to stay on. It was applied with a fine black inkpen, but it stained my skin and stayed on for days afterwards!'

In her other roles, Judy has the on-screen distinction of taking the virginity of two soap characters – Mark Hughes in *Emmerdale*, in which she played Paula Barker, and Andy McDonald in *Coronation Street*, when she was cast as Paula Maxwell.

In *Peak Practice*, Judy's mother, Cath, was played by **Anna Keaveney**, best known as battleaxe Marie Jackson in *Brookside*. She also acted a council leader in writer Jimmy McGovern's powerful drugs drama *Needle*, and made a brief appearance as April Brooks, mother of Archie, in *Emmerdale*.

Rebecca Dawson (Judy Brooke) shows Will the tatoo on her arm before he discovers the infected one on her back.

cleaned it up and gave Rebecca the encouragement and support she needed to tell her mother that she was giving up her library job after all and going to art college in Nottingham. With Will's help, mother and daughter had found a better understanding, with Rebecca telling Cath that she wanted no more secrets.

BETH GRIEVES FOR ISABEL

Beth was dealt a devastating blow when her best friend, Isabel de Gines, died of pancreatic cancer, leaving a gaping hole in Beth's life. Isabel had always been there with her 'no frills' advice or a glass of whisky to cry into.

Beth bravely faced up to Isabel's funeral and threw a wake at her own home. After the last of the guests had paid their respects and left, Beth came across a letter addressed to her as she sorted through a pile of Isabel's correspondence.

She wept as she read Isabel's advice from the grave. Direct to the last, she wrote that Beth and Jack should get on with starting a family – advice that Beth was keen to follow. She felt the time was right for her and Jack to plan a child, although he remained a little reluctant, feeling there was plenty of time to think about babies.

Isabel de Gines confides her cancer to Beth, who faces up to a future without the friend who has always been there for her.

JACK COMES UNDER FIRE

Beth was to have her plans for a family threatened by an incident that left Jack so disillusioned that he left for a sabbatical in Africa in order to collect his thoughts.

When Amanda Stokes went into premature labour in a cornfield after a car accident, Jack stepped in to deliver her baby. The umbilical cord was wound tightly round the baby's neck, so Jack released it before an ambulance arrrived to take the infant to hospital. At the hospital, Amanda and husband Mark were told that their son had suffered two small fits and might have brain damage. They blamed Jack and lodged a complaint of medical negligence, claiming that Jack had panicked and taken too long to remove the umbilical cord – a fact that Jack disputed.

When the case was set to go before a disciplinary hearing, Jack became headline news in the local papers and patients at The Beeches began to transfer to the health centre. But the complaint was later dropped when tests on the baby revealed calcification of the brain caused by the foetus becoming infected with toxoplasmosis while still in the womb. The infant's father, Mark, had worked on a farm during the lambing season where he might have picked up the parasites that are the cause of the illness.

At the height of these events, Jack had met up with his old friend Francine Sinclair, with

Jack is unaware of what is to come later when a car crash sends Amanda Stokes (Kate O'Malley) into premature labour.

In Africa, Jack escapes his troubles but comes to realise that his home is now in Cardale with Beth.

whom he had worked at the Dry River Clinic in Zimbabwe. She asked Jack if he would return there to help her to set up an outreach programme at the clinic. With a bitter taste in his mouth, and feeling that Cardale had turned its back on him, Jack decided – against Beth's wishes – to go back to the country where he had once felt so at home.

TROUBLESHOOTING IN AFRICA

Following Isabel's death, Beth was extremely troubled when Jack left for Africa and feared that her husband would always run away when he had problems. While she was left to cope at home, he immersed himself in his work, overwhelmed by the multitude of people who arrived at the clinic for measle vaccinations and Vitamin A shots, which help to prevent blindness.

As supplies ran dangerously low, Jack decided to collect the urgent medication that lay trapped by bureaucracy in a warehouse 200 miles away. With a little Kerruish charm, he persuaded a government official to release the Vitamin A.

Jack felt valued in Africa and had time to work out how he really felt about Beth, Cardale and a baby. After two months, he bade a tearful farewell to Francine, who was keen for Jack to remain in Africa. He told her that he could not stay, because he would grow to hate the country that kept him away from Beth. It was time to go home and start a family with the woman he loved.

Jack arrived back in Cardale to a warm welcome from The Beeches staff. Although over the moon to have him home, Beth still needed reasurance that he was there to stay. Once she had this, to Jack's amusement, Beth drew up an ovulation chart rather than let nature take its course, and marked key days with a red star.

CLOUD WITH A SILVER LINING

Pensioner Edna Sturgess, laid up in bed awaiting a hip revision operation, was totally reliant on her husband, Frank, who himself suffered from angina. Although he tried his best, 78-year-old Edna never seemed satisfied and her condition was putting a strain on their marriage.

When Edna developed a bed sore that had a highly contagious multi-resistant staphylococcus aureus infection, no hospital would touch her until it had healed, which could take some months. At the end of his tether, Frank stormed out of the house after a row with his wife.

Alone at night, Edna fell and fractured her thigh bone while making a drink. Practice nurse Laura Elliott discovered her the following morning and called an ambulance. A distressed Frank was delighted to find that, because Edna had been admitted as an emergency, she would get her hip operation straight away.

> • Pensioner Edna Sturgess, awaiting a hip operation, was played by **Jean Heywood**, previously seen as Bella Seaton in *When the Boat Comes In*, Dolly Skilbeck's mother, Phyllis Acaster, in *Emmerdale*, Dolly McGregor in T*he Brothers McGregor* and Aunt Dahlia in *Jeeves and Wooster*. She has since acted Sally Hart in the Channel 5 soap *Family Affairs*.

SUICIDE ATTEMPT

Cardale farmer Tim Shardlow had been suffering from depression since his wife, Maggie, had died. Beth was reluctant to give him a repeat prescription when his antidepressants ran out and made an appointment for him to see her at The Beeches.

That evening, Tim arrived dressed to the nines for a supper date with Chloë and James White at The Manor Hotel. He was clutching a bundle of photographs, some flowers for Chloë and a pair of Maggie's earrings to be given to their daugher, Sarah-Jane, when she became a woman. Tim grew drunk and melancholy as he pored over his wedding album and holiday snaps. Declining an invitation to stay the night, he walked home in the early hours.

Tim had lost the will to live. After leaving a note, feeding the dog and placing a jug of fresh flowers on the shelf under the photograph he kept of Maggie, Tim attempted to take his own life by feeding the fumes from the exhaust pipe of his Land Rover into the sealed cab through an attached hosepipe.

Concerned about his failure to keep his appointment at the surgery, Beth arrived at the farm, smashed the garage doors down with one of Tim's farm vehicles and dragged him out. Later, in hospital, Tim verbally attacked Beth for interfering and warned her that he would succeed next time.

MOTHER DRINKS TO FORGET

Pauline Wadham was an alcoholic, who, in violent rages, stabbed and hit her carpenter husband John. Eventually, the couple sought help from Will, who promised to get Pauline the help she needed after she admitted to drinking a bottle of spirits a day for the past two years. She wanted to blot out the pain she felt over the death of her five-year-old son, Sam, who had been killed by a truck.

• Royal Shakespeare Company actor **Graham Turner** played husband-beating victim John Wadham before going on to act Edward 'Binny' Edwards in the prison series *Insiders*, also written by *Peak Practice*'s creator Lucy Gannon. In real life, Graham was already the boyfriend of Jacqueline Leonard, who acted Will Preston's wife, Sarah.

WILL HAS A FLING

The ink was hardly dry on Will's divorce papers when he started seeing Janey Cooper, a bubbly blonde drugs rep, although Will described her as 'a no strings sort of girl' to Beth and complained that she was nothing like Sarah.

Their affair finally bit the dust when Will's son Tony was nearly paralysed in a rugby accident. Will, standing on the touchline positively bursting with pride, had taken Janey to Royston School to watch his

eldest son take part in a rugby tournament. Tragedy struck when a rough tackle left Tony lying unconscious on the pitch with a serious neck injury.

Frantic, Will called for an ambulance and stood and wept openly as Tony was carried off the field on a stretcher. When he regained conciousness at the hospital, both Will and ex-wife Sarah were at his bedside, with Janey taking care of their other son, Julian. The sexy young rep, seeing Will the family man for the first time, decided that such scenes of domesticity were not for her and beat a hasty retreat.

Drugs rep Janey Cooper (Sasha Paul) brings some much needed sparkle into Will's life.

Tony, who had been paralysed since the accident, slowly regained the feeling in his legs and eventually moved back into Will's home with Sarah while they both nursed him back to health. The accident seemed to have drawn the couple closer and they almost resumed their married sleeping arrangements after a happy day celebrating Julian's birthday.

Despite the renewed warmth between them, Will couldn't forget that he had been to hell and back with Sarah and he didn't want to make the journey again. After leaving Sarah for a fabricated emergency call-out, she came to the same conclusion. She moved out and, although the pair were free to begin their lives once again, Will found himself battling with jealousy when he was introduced to Sarah's new boyfriend, Michael Poole.

Robbo's challenge to an illegal bare-knuckle fight for money. Meanwhile Will searched frantically for him to give him the good news about the brain scan and the treatment he so urgently needed for his condition. Will stepped in to stop the fight and received a black eye for his efforts. On being taken home, Pete was assured that, to protect his amateur status, nothing would be mentioned about the illegal fight.

- Irene Brodie, who saw her boxer son Pete black out, was acted by **Melanie Kiburn**, previously seen as Jill in *Making Out*, Carol in the first series of *Soldier Soldier*, Barbara Bibby in *The Lifeboat* and Charlotte in the sitcom *Moving Story*. In the same episode, **Gaynor Faye** appeared once more as WPC Benson before going on to act Judy Mallett in *Coronation Street*.

BOXER'S TOUGHEST FIGHT

Pete Brodie, a young Cardale boxer with his sights set firmly on Olympic selection one day, busily prepared for his latest match in the East Midlands Amateur Boxing Association championship, with Will acting as the ABA medical adviser.

After being floored at the end of a training session by his sparring partner, Robbo Gibbs, Pete hid his blurred vision and blackouts from Will, and concentrated on losing weight quickly to qualify for the fight. But Will was called when the young boxer blacked out in front of his mother, Irene. A scan revealed no brain damage, but a blood test showed that Pete was suffering from hypoglycaemia – low blood sugar – caused by excessive dieting.

Convinced that his days as a champion amateur boxer were over, Pete accepted

Pete Brodie (Thomas Aldwinckle) resorts to a bare-knuckle fight when he thinks his career is over, but Will steps in to give him the news that he does not have brain damage.

MOTHER AND SON REUNITED

Nancy Thurston was a middle-aged woman who suffered from Huntington's disease, a rare hereditary illness affecting the nervous system and muscles. She lived out her days in a nursing home, her agile mind trapped in a body that jerked this way and that, out of control. When she attempted suicide by pushing her hands though a glass window and slashing her wrists, Jack rushed to patch her up and had her transferred to The Templeton, a psychiatric unit that could provide the round-the-clock care she so desperately needed.

Jack, set on a little social work, discovered from Nancy's sister, Jean, that she had an illegitimate son called Doug, who had been fostered when the authorities, unaware of her disease, mistook her symptoms for antisocial behaviour and took her child from her.

When Jack tracked down Doug, he was bitter that his mother had given him away, as he saw it, and angry that the GP had waltzed into his life and dropped the bombshell that he might develop Huntington's disease himself. Struggling to come to terms with the news, Doug eventually agreed to undergo tests for the condition after six months of genetic counselling. He also visited the unit to see his mother for the first time since he was a child. Nancy recognised him immediately and her face lit up with a broad smile.

• **Julia Ford**, who played Liz Thurston, daughter-in-law of Huntington's disease sufferer Nancy, has since taken the roles of Dr Liz Seymour in *Medics* and workshop manager Annie Whitby in Lucy Gannon's prison series *Insiders*.

A matron seen in the same episode was acted by **Marlene Sidaway**, previously seen in *Coronation Street* as the mother of Curly Watts's ex-fiancée, Kimberley Taylor. She has since played Hill in the serial *Pride and Prejudice* and Dee Yearwood in the series *Accused*.

STORMY TIMES IN CARDALE

Trees, telephone lines and electricity were down in Cardale as high winds and flash flooding wreaked havoc, with many residents being evacuated from their homes and finding safety in the church.

A quiz by candlelight was in progress at The Manor Hotel, where Liverpudlian newcomer Marian Daley was helping out behind the bar. She had left her jailbird husband in prison and escaped to Cardale with her asthmatic teenaged son, Sean, to make a fresh start. But, as Marian worked, Sean made a bungled attempt at car theft, lost his inhaler in the panic and was having trouble getting his breath. Later, he broke into The Manor Hotel and made

• Being clobbered by a burglar in *Peak Practice* brought back embarrassing memories for Richard Platt, who plays The Manor Hotel landlord James White and in real life lives with former *Coronation Street* actress Tracy Brabin.

'A couple of years ago, Tracy and I were walking through Covent Garden when someone came up behind us and grabbed her,' Richard recalls. 'I swung round and walloped him with my briefcase, giving him a fat nose and a lot of pain. My immediate reaction was to protect her.

'Then Tracy realised that it was a friend of mine and he said he was just trying to surprise us. I was so embarrassed!'

off with the takings, dealing landlord James White a nasty crack to the head in the process.

Shortly afterwards, Beth was called to assist Sean, who had collapsed with a chronic asthma attack. Spotting his bag of bootie, she realised that Sean was James's assailant. He confessed that he had taken the money to care for his pregnant 16-year-old girlfriend.

Beth tends Manor landlord James White after he is clubbed by Sean Daley, who made off with the pub takings.

With no sign of an ambulance coming, Jack and Beth drove James and Sean to hospital in Derby in Will's Range Rover. When a tree crashed in their path, they narrowly escaped being crushed. An ambulance eventually reached them, but it was too late for Sean, who died. James went on to make a full recovery.

ROMANCE FOR KIM

Romance was in the air for practice manager Kim Beardsmore after she attended her old school reunion. She had been reluctant to attend, but had gone along at the insistence of her former teacher Roy Shearer.

When she met Alec Kitson, whom she remembered from her school days for his tearaway antics, she was glad she had. He was now on the straight and narrow, making his living as a landscape gardener. An unlikley pair, Alec had a heart of gold and began to win Kim over with kindness to her son, Sam.

TEACHER'S PET – OR LOVER?

• Roy Shearer, the teacher who was victim of a schoolgirl crush, was played by **Richard Hope**, who has appeared in many television plays, as well as playing Mortimer Tundish in *The Riff Raff Element*, Stuart Freeman in *Tears Before Bedtime*, Geraldine James's boyfriend, Richard, in *Band of Gold*, and MP Simon Watson in *A Perfect State*.

Dee Sadler, the actress wife of *Casualty* star Derek Thompson, played Claire Davis, who was the mother of schoolgirl Josie, who had a crush on her teacher. Dee had previously acted Tracy Crabtree in the sitcom *No Place Like Home* and has also been seen in *Pie in the Sky* and *The Bill*.

Bright 13-year-old schoolgirl Josie Davis began to suffer from hallucinations, and could no longer distinguish between fact and fiction when school bullies claimed that form teacher Roy Shearer was really her lover. In fact, the other girls were jealous of the extra attention that he gave to Josie because he was so pleased to be teaching such an enthusiastic pupil.

One day, after Josie had been left alone in the house caring for her baby brother, her parents returned to find the baby screaming and Josie writhing around on the kitchen floor in agony after scalding herself with a pan of hot water.

Her wounds were treated at The Beeches by Will, who was told of Alan and Claire Davis's concern for their daughter. Will was shocked when Josie claimed that her teacher had told her that he loved her and that he would not leave her alone. Will went to the school to see Roy, who had been at The Beeches on the same day being treated for stress by Beth. He denied that there was anything improper between him and Josie.

Malicious playground gossip about Josie being pregnant with Roy's child then came to the attention of her father. He warned Roy to keep away from his daughter, then returned home and rowed with his wife. Josie ran away, unable to cope with the problems she was causing and terrified that she was going mad. Her father and Will eventually found her having a full-blown fit in the graveyard. Will's examination revealed a form of epilepsy and Josie was taken to hospital for further tests. Although no longer under suspicion, Roy decided to leave the school, feeling that a teacher's job had changed too much over the years.

BROUGHT TO BOOK

Soldier Gary Donalds visited Jack with excrutiating stomach pains caused by old shrapnel wounds, a legacy from his days in Northern Ireland. Gary refused to go to hospital for urgent treatment, claiming that he had been AWOL for the past two years after beating up his NCO, who had called him a coward.

When the military police tracked Gary down to The Beeches through his National Health Service number, they revealed that he was actually charged with murder. After going into hiding, Gary ended up banging at Jack's front door in the middle of the night when he was unable to cope with the pain. Jack explained that without urgent medical attention he would die, and persuaded Gary to hand himself over.

A TRAINEE ARRIVES

Beth, Will and Jack decided to invite trainee GP Dr Andrew Attwood to join The Beeches for six months. Although the most inexperienced doctor on the team, the Liverpudlian had worked in several city hospital departments over the previous year.

He soon began to settle in Cardale, despite being parted from his wife, Kirsty, back in Liverpool. Jack acted as Andrew's mentor, guiding him through the sensitive issue of patient-doctor relations. Andrew appeared brash at times but, with Jack's help, the rough edges soon began to be worn down.

Like other Beeches doctors before him, Andrew first lodged at The Manor Hotel pub before moving out to stay temporarily with practice nurse Laura Elliott when Chloë and James White decided to foster a child.

Trainee GP Andrew Attwood (Gary Mavers) joins The Beeches for six months, but his undiplomatic style causes problems.

ANDREW LOSES CONTRACT

On Andrew's first day at The Beeches, he was taken to the local tannery by Jack, the plant's medical officer. A shocked Andrew told tannery owner Roger Wyatt that it was unwise, and illegal, to let his 15-year-old son, Terry, work there alongside the heavy machinery. As a result, Roger cancelled his medical contract with The Beeches, which displeased fund manager Trevor Sharp, incensed that Andrew had lost the practice a deal worth £3,000 a year.

A tragedy saved the day when Will and Andrew were later called to the tannery to assist Roger, who had become trapped in one of his machines. With Terry's help, Andrew, who was a former electrician, managed to dismantle the

• Actor-writer **Bob Mason**, who played tannery boss Roger Wyatt, had acted Terry Bradshaw, brother of Alf Roberts's second wife, Rene, in *Coronation Street*, before going on to write episodes of the serial.

machine and save Roger's arm.

After the accident, Roger had a change of heart and retracted his decision to cancel the tannery's medical contract. He also admitted that the plant was not the best place for Terry to work and promised that his son would not be working there again.

JACK AND BETH'S HEARTBREAK

Jack and Beth were overjoyed when Beth fell pregnant. Although she suffered from terrible morning sickness, nothing could dampen the happiness that Beth felt. She relished the collection of tiny clothes she had been accumulating and began to turn their spare room into a nursery.

However, their happiness was cut short when Beth suffered a miscarriage one night. Heartbroken, she retreated into a world of her own and concentrated on work. Jack needed Beth more than ever, but she kept him at arm's length.

Jack comforts Beth after her miscarriage but finds their relationship strained when she retreats into her own world.

• Rose Godfrey, who needed surgery for an aneurysm while coming to terms with Dr Andrew Attwood prescribing the Pill for her 15-year-old daughter, was played by **Jo Kendall**, best known as Peggy Skilbeck in the early days of *Emmerdale*. She has also guest-starred in series such as *Second Thoughts*, *Searching*, *Oliver's Travels* and *The Bill*.

A MOTHER'S WRATH

God-fearing Catholic Rose Godfrey had raised her three children and run her own riding stables since the death of her husband. While sons Matthew and Dominic attended Derby Technical College and her 15-year-old daughter,

Kate, was at school, Rose worked in the stables with Kate's 17-year-old boyfriend, Mark, whom she employed as a stable lad.

Ill with angina for some time, Rose took the advice of Beth, a friend and riding companion, and visited The Beeches for a checkup. Andrew was the only doctor available to see her, and Jack was angry to find out that he had changed Rose's medication without giving her a proper examination. At Rose's home, the pair gave her a full examination and detected signs of an aneurysm in her aorta, which meant going to hospital for further tests.

Meanwhile, daughter Kate had asked Andrew to prescribe the contraceptive Pill, but he urged her to think again. However, when Kate and her boyfriend, Mark, arrived together in his surgery a couple of days later, he decided they were both mature enough to know what they were doing, and prescribed the Pill. When Rose discovered Kate's concealed pack of pills, she banished Kate to her room, fired Mark and lashed out at Jack, and hardly seemed to absorb the news that she needed to undergo surgery for her aneurysm.

When Rose collapsed in her highly emotional state, an ambulance was called to whisk her to hospital. Beth and Andrew remained to care for the three children, but Kate – blaming herself for her mother's collapse – gave them the slip and drove herself to the hospital to be with her mother. Jack greeted her with the good news that Rose had undergone a successful operation and was on the road to recovery. Reunited with her daughter, Rose apologised for overreacting and gave Mark his job back. Kate decided to wait until she was older before embarking on a sexual relationship.

MISCARRIAGE OF JUSTICE?

Joe Rawlings returned home to his parents' Cardale fish-and-chip shop in a final attempt to kick his heroin habit. When his GP, Dr John Reginald at the Brompton Health Centre, refused to treat him because of his past track record of failure, Joe could do nothing but suffer the agonies of 'cold turkey'.

• Heroin-addicted teenager Joe Rawlings was played by **Chris Gascoyne**, who has since taken the roles of Fusilier Tony Rossi in *Soldier Soldier* and Barry Forrester in *The Locksmith*. His mother, Doreen, was played by **Stephanie Turner**, best known as Inspector Jean Darblay in the first three series of *Juliet Bravo*. She has also played Miss Armitage in the sitcom *The Hello Girls* and guest-starred in programmes such as *Boon*, *Van Der Valk*, *Casualty*, *The Bill* and *A Touch of Frost*.

After an evening at The Manor Hotel, a drunk Joe vomited on a parked car before putting his elbow through the window. When police took him to the station, Beth was called out to treat Joe. He told Beth that he felt responsible for the drug overdose of his flatmate, Tony, while he himself had been 'out of it'. This incident had convinced Joe that it was time to give up. Beth agreed to take him on as a patient but, when she refused to give him any methadone until he had sobered up, he made a dash at Beth's bag, knocking her into the wall as he did so.

Beth suffered her miscarriage only hours after the incident, but this later turned out to be pure coincidence. The next time Joe turned up at The Beeches, Jack refused to take him on as a patient, offering him a referral to a drugs unit at the hospital instead. Running to his parents' shop, Joe stole a wad of notes from the till to score some heroin. He was later found semiconscious by Beth, who had called round to apologise for Jack's behaviour.

Rushed to hospital, Joe was found to have injected purer heroin than he was used to. Beth reassured Joe that he had not been responsible for the loss of her baby and offered him the chance to break his habit by accepting treatment at The Beeches.

CHANGE OF DIAGNOSIS

David Frankland took a paracetamol overdose and stabbed himself with a carpet knife before stumbling into The Beeches after his wife, Gill, had walked out on him, taking Melanie, her child by a previous relationship, with her. Her departure had been precipitated by the discovery that he had concealed six months of unpaid bills in the back of a sofa cushion. Andrew and Beth rushed David to hospital, where his wounds were tended before he was assessed by the duty psychiatrist, Dr Mike Nelson. Seeing the incident as a cry for help, the psychiatrist discharged him.

On finding out about David's mounting debts and threat of house repossession, Andrew believed he was suffering from reactive depression, which is caused by external circumstances. The doctor persuaded Chloë and James at The Manor Hotel to pay David to decorate their function room. But, when Gill refused to return to him despite his brighter prospects, David arrived at The Manor Hotel drunk.

Desperately missing Melanie, he confusedly took young Sarah-Jane White for a ride to the builder's yard, believing her to be his stepdaughter. When David returned, a scuffle broke out between him and James, who had been sick with worry. Realising that David was probably suffering from schizophrenia, Andrew called in a psychiatrist, who confirmed his diagnosis. As a result, David was sectioned and sent to hospital for treatment.

WILL WAKES UP

Without realising it, Andrew's presence had made Will dissatisfied with his own career. Feeling that he had stagnated, he applied and was accepted for a part-time position as a clinical assistant in the ENT department at Derby Royal Infirmary. Once Beth had recovered from her intial disappointment at not being told, she realised that The Beeches could benefit from the expertise that Will was gaining.

She thought Will would be thrilled when Trevor gave the go-ahead for a new outreach clinic to be built on to The Beeches. Instead, he told Beth and Jack that he disagreed with their plans because they would take important funding from hospitals. He stunned them further by revealing that he had been offered, but had not yet accepted, a new job as medical adviser to the North Riding Health Authority.

A RISK TOO FAR

Life was tough on the dole, but Dougie Greaves did what he could to make it bearable for his family, taking whatever work he was offered. For several seasons, he helped with sheep dipping at Grogan's Farm, and he was now trying to save enough money to buy his wife, Tina, a china figurine for her birthday.

He seemed to be suffering from persistent flu, so Tina and his son, Toby, persuaded him to see the doctor. When Beth asked Dougie to produce a urine specimen, he emerged from the toilet 15 minutes later in pain and complaining of distorted vision. Later, he fell down the stairs, smashing his wife's present as he did so.

Beth discovered that Dougie had been seeing Dr Daniel Acres and had a history of sporadic respiratory problems. Despite this, he had not attended any of the tests that had been arranged for him.

Dougie's troubles continued when, while dismantling a barn for a local farmer with Toby, Dougie let go of a pulley, sending the barn roof crashing down around them, narrowly missing his son. Then, during a karaoke night at The Manor Hotel, Dougie fell into a fit of muscle spasms on stage.

When Beth called on the family the next day, Tina finally admitted that Dougie had been involved in sheep dipping. Beth went

• **Lorraine Ashbourne**, sister of actress Jayne, played Tina Greaves, whose husband, Dougie, suffered pesticide poisoning after taking work dipping a farmer's sheep. She has also appeared in *Pie in the Sky*, the 'Chiller' story *Number Six, Life's a Bitch* and *The Bill*. In the same episode, Monika Gaye – whose talk during a weekend fostering course was attended by James and Chloë White – was acted by *Beverley Hills*, who later played Elaine Johnson in *Brookside*.

to see Grogan, the farmer, and she was horrified to learn that none of the labourers had worn protective clothing while using the toxic chemicals. After Beth told the farmer that she had no choice but to report him for illegal practices, he laid Dougie off.

An angry Dougie told Beth that she had no right to interfere and that he had known the risks he faced. Beth then explained that hospital test results showed that he had suffered irreparable damage to his nervous system and internal organs caused by organophosphate poisoning.

CHLOE AND JAMES FOSTER

With her cancer still in remission, The Manor Hotel landlady Chloë White was able to put her health worries behind her and look to the future with husband James and daughter Sarah-Jane.

The couple knew they had a lot to offer more than one child and decided that, with Chloë no longer able to have another of her own, they would like to foster. After attending various training days and interviews, the Whites welcomed eight-year-old Matthew into their home as their first foster child.

COMPLICATED
LOVE TRIANGLE

Newly qualified solicitor Vanessa Machin was a cystic fibrosis sufferer living with her overprotective sister and brother-in-law, Louise and Martin Beckham, who were about to embark on an in vitro fertilisation (IVF) programme in an attempt to have a child of their own.

When Vanessa announced that she wanted to leave for a flat of her own, Louise was frightened that Vanessa would be unable to cope as her condition steadily deteriorated. Unknown to Louise, her husband had been having an affair with Vanessa and she wanted a flat so that she and Martin could spend more time alone together, grabbing what happiness she could in the short time left to her.

Jack, who was approached for a housing association reference by Vanessa and who

saw her kissing Martin outside The Manor Hotel, confided in Beth. She was angry that the Beckhams should even be considering the IVF programme when they did not have a stable marriage.

Beth finally agreed to refer the couple for IVF treatment after Louise told her that she had known about Vanessa and Martin's affair for some time, but that she tolerated it because their relationship was no real threat to her marriage. However, Martin decided to end his affair with Vanessa after she moved into her flat.

JACK AND BETH
FACE THE FUTURE

Beth's miscarriage had made her restless. When Will announced that he was leaving The Beeches to take up his new post in Yorkshire, she almost envied him, telling Jack that she had never meant to live in Cardale for ever.

However, Will changed his mind about the new job at the eleventh hour, after pensioner Alice North made him realise that he belonged in Cardale. Beth grabbed the opportunity to cure her wanderlust. For the first time since her miscarriage, she felt vibrant and alive.

She told Jack that they couldn't shake off their pain because they were both stuck in the past. She felt that they needed to find themselves and believed they could do this in Africa. As Jack and Beth planned a six-month sabbatical, Will agreed to take charge of The Beeches and Andrew looked forward to working as his locum.

> • Cystic fibrosis sufferer Vanessa Machin was played by **Susannah Corbett**, daughter of *Steptoe and Son* star Harry H Corbett. She has since played Ellie Soper, who married Det. Sgt Peter Pascoe, in the detective series *Dalziel and Pascoe*.
>
> In *Peak Practice*, her screen sister's husband, Martin, was played by **Jo Dow** who, as Jonathan Dow, had acted PC Barry Stringer in *The Bill*. He is also known for his role as Dr James Mortimer in three series of *Cardiac Arrest*.
>
> In the same episode, David Cornish – The Beeches' solicitor who drew up a document allowing for Will's planned departure from the practice – was played by **John D Collins**, best known as Flying Officer Fairfax in *'Allo, 'Allo* and Jerry in *You Rang, M'Lord?*

WHO'S WHO IN CARDALE

DR JACK KERRUISH
(Kevin Whately)

• With a broken marriage and a failed relationship behind him, as well as three years of living a dream by setting up a clinic in Zimbabwe, Jack brought his own charismatic style to Cardale as a partner in The Beeches, helping it to modernise in the face of competition from the new Brompton Health Centre. He also showed himself to be a caring GP, who constantly fought against injustice. In his quest to put patients first, Jack shared much with senior partner Beth Glover, but his idealism sometimes got the better of him.

The kindred spirit he found in Beth led them to marry, but a complaint of negligence against Jack – although eventually dropped – led him to leave for a break in Zimbabwe to reassess his life and help at the clinic that had once held so many happy memories for him.

Coming to realise that his home was in Cardale with Beth, Jack returned to start a family but was heartbroken when his wife miscarried. However, he returned to Africa – with Beth – when the couple decided it was time to leave behind their life in Cardale and look to the future.

DR BETH GLOVER
(Amanda Burton)

DR WILL PRESTON
(Simon Shepherd)

• After inheriting The Beeches from her father, senior partner Beth faced the prospect of having to replace Dr Daniel Acres when he was poached by the new health centre, which was a threat to her own practice. She found it difficult to talk of patients and business in the same breath, but was forced to face up to economic reality and took on Dr Jack Kerruish to help her ensure The Beeches' survival.

They shared a stubborn streak that ensured a fiery relationship, but Beth was immediately attracted to the unconventional GP, who brought a breath of fresh air into her life. She tried to resist, but eventually she fell for his charms and became his wife. At the practice, she also resisted fund-holding until it became a reality of the times.

Two incidents led to Beth's departure from Cardale. First, her close friend Isabel de Gines died of cancer, leaving a huge gap in the GP's life. Then, after the joy of falling pregnant with Jack's baby, she miscarried. Feeling that they were stuck in the past, Beth told Jack that she wanted to move forward and she thought that his beloved Africa might be the place to make a fresh start. They went on a six-month sabbatical and never returned after deciding to stay and buy into the Johannesburg clinic they had gone to work at.

• Public schoolboy Will was junior partner in The Beeches when Jack Kerruish arrived. Married to Sarah, he found it difficult to meet her financial demands. Eventually, he had a nervous breakdown. As he and Sarah tried to make a new start, they moved into a smaller house with their two sons, Tony and Julian, but their relationship did not improve and Sarah eventually walked out.

Still reeling from the break-up, Will had a short fling with drugs rep Janey Cooper, then was almost reunited with Sarah when together they nursed son Tony back to health following an accident on the rugby field. But Sarah left, and Will had to contend with her emigrating to America with his sons and her new boyfriend.

When Jack and Beth left for Africa, Will found himself as senior partner at The Beeches. At the same time, new love came into his life with the arrival of Dr Kate Webster at the rival health centre. On becoming pregnant, she decided against her initial instinct to get rid of the baby. After Emily was born, Will and Kate were shocked to discover that she was suffering from cystic fibrosis. Eventually, they married and moved to Bristol so that the baby could be part of a research programme that might improve her quality of life.

ISABEL DE GINES
(Sylvia Syms)

• Local magistrate and long-time Cardale resident and friend of the Glover family, widow Isabel was Beth's confidante. She strongly supported Beth in taking on Jack Kerruish in her professional and private life. She herself had short romances with a widower called Gerard and dye factory boss Ken Alton.

Isabel resigned from the bench after an unsympathetic magistrate sentenced drug user Carl Clarke to a spell in prison, despite his genuine desire to join a drug rehabilitation centre. It was a terrible shock to best friend Beth when Isabel, whose forthright, no-frills advice she had found so invaluable, died of pancreatic cancer in 1995.

SARAH PRESTON
(Jacqueline Leonard)

• Trying to leave her working-class roots behind, Sarah liked the idea of being married to a country GP and enjoying a luxury life style. Unfortunately, with sons Tony and Julian at private school, her own financial demands threatened to bankrupt the family. Frustrated at Will's lack of ambition, she had an affair with Dr Daniel Acres in an attempt to secure Will a partnership at the new health centre.

Will warned Acres off, but little improved in his marriage. After Will suffered a breakdown, Sarah went along with his attempts to make a new start, moving to a smaller house with him and taking a school secretary's job. However, there was no love left in their marriage and Sarah eventually left Will.

When son Tony was injured in a rugby accident, Sarah returned, but the couple realised that there was no future for them together. Later, Sarah took her sons to America to start again with her new boyfriend.

KIM BEARDSMORE
(Esther Coles)

• Fiercely loyal, Beeches receptionist Kim had lived in Cardale all her life and was a single mother with a son called Sam. The father initially stuck by her but soon decided that he was too young to settle down. She was made practice manager after Jack Kerruish's arrival and the installation of a new computer system.

Kim put in many extra hours of work to help Will Preston put together all the data needed to make The Beeches a fundholding practice, and was disappointed when she was not appointed fund manager, although she did work for a while as assistant fund manager. She found short-lived romances with former school friend Alec Kitson and practice fund manager Russ Skinner.

ELLIE NDEBALA
(Sharon Hinds)

• The Beeches' original practice nurse, Ellie was brought up in Derbyshire, 'the only black face for miles', after her Ghanaian parents gave her up for adoption to a white couple. She suffered an identity crisis, feeling that she was neither white nor black. Overly sensitive as a result, she snapped at Jack for dressing one of her patients' leg ulcers after his arrival following three years in Africa.

JAMES and
CHLOE WHITE
(Richard Platt and
Hazel Ellerby)

• The Manor Hotel pub landlord and landlady, James and Chloë, were ecstatic when daughter Sarah-Jane was born in 1993 after Chloë received fertility treatment following years of problems in conceiving. It was subsequently a devastating blow when Chloë learned that she had Hodgkin's disease, but she and James were relieved when Jack Kerruish announced that her cancer was in remission following a course of chemotherapy.

The couple stopped renting rooms out when they were taken on as foster carers by social services in 1995. Their first foster child was eight-year-old Matthew and they later took in teenager Gary Simms, who was joined at The Manor Hotel by his elder brother, Lee. Daughter Sarah-Jane's heart surgery in 1996, after her fourth birthday party, caused James and Chloë much anxiety, but surgery to repair a damaged heart valve was successful.

**ALICE NORTH
(Margery Mason)**

**DR ANDREW
ATTWOOD
(Gary Mavers)**

• Irascible old soul Alice North, whose husband died from stomach cancer, had a gruff exterior but a heart of gold. She suffered gall bladder problems, agoraphobia, carbon monoxide poisoning and a hip operation.

Her most constant companions were her chickens, but she was close to war veteran Douglas Hart until his death and, more recently, formed an alliance with pensioner Alby James. She was also a firm friend of Dr Will Shepherd and persuaded him not to leave The Beeches for a job as medical adviser to the North Riding Health Authority.

• Andrew arrived at The Beeches from Liverpool as a trainee in 1995 and was taken on by Will as a locum when he was deserted by Jack and Beth. He had come to medicine late, inspired to leave his job as an electrician after his father, a steel worker, died early from pneumoconiosis, a work-related lung condition. Andrew was supported financially through medical school by wife Kirsty and began to leave his working-class roots behind.

When Erica Matthews joined The Beeches, Andrew found himself looked over for a partnership. He also faced personal problems when his wife left him to return to Liverpool. Suffering a nervous breakdown, Andrew walked out on Will and Erica as he was finally about to become a partner and worked in a Manchester inner-city practice for six months.

Returning to Cardale in 1997, he was eventually taken back into the fold as a partner. However, he tangled stethoscopes with the other doctors when he over-enthusiastically tried to implement cost-saving measures. Andrew also tangled with Erica on a personal level, although their romance was an on-off affair. In 1998, Erica finally said she would marry him and the couple headed for the altar, only for Erica to jilt Andrew on their wedding day.

DR ERICA MATTHEWS
(Saskia Wickham)

DR DAVID SHEARER
(Adrian Lukis)

• After growing up in Leicestershire, and working as a trainee, then locum, in a Manchester inner-city practice, Erica left following the break-up of her relationship with boyfriend Dan Copeland and took a locum's job at The Beeches. It took her a while to adjust to life in the Peak District, but she settled in and became a partner.

Stability was important to Erica. Having been adopted at the age of six, she was vulnerable and seemed to need affection, but would face hurt and rejection in her quest to find it. She had a crush on Will Preston, but he fell for Kate Webster and, after sleeping the night with Andrew Attwood, she was met the following morning by his guilt and remorse.

However, Erica sent old flame Dan Copeland packing after he arrived in Cardale. She admitted her feelings for Andrew, but told him that he would have to wait for any commitment until she had tracked down her natural parents. Erica met her real father, Geordie trucker Jackie Brown, and discovered that her mother had died. Then, in 1998, she proposed to Andrew and they organised a church wedding, but Erica jilted him on the day and left Cardale for good.

• Born in the neighbouring village of Braisewell, David worked in the practice there after training at medical school in Nottingham, before marrying Spanish wife Clare and moving to Sheffield, then Portsmouth. Completely devoted to his patients, who find him reassuring and trustworthy, he hates the fact that doctors are forced to think like accountants. As such, he was opposed to fundholding, but accepted the opportunity to return to Derbyshire when Will Preston, a friend from medical school, offered him a job in 1997 as a locum at The Beeches. When Will left, David became a partner.

In the surgery, David frequently found

himself clashing with Andrew Attwood, who was a supporter of fundholding and over-enthusiastically set about cost-cutting. At home, David – who has two children, Emma and Tom – coped with wife Clare's manic depression just three years after she experienced a nervous breakdown.

It was a shock to David when Clare fell pregnant and had to choose whether to have an abortion or come off the drugs that were controlling her depression. They decided to go ahead with the pregnancy and son William was born without placing any undue stress on Clare.

DR KATE WEBSTER
(Shelagh McLeod)

CLARE SHEARER
(Yolanda Vazquez
and Fiona Gillies)

• Arriving in Cardale in 1996, Nottingham-born Dr Kate Webster – divorced from GP husband Greg – turned down Will Preston's offer of a partnership at The Beeches in favour of joining the Brompton Health Centre, following Dr John Reginald's departure. However, she fell for Will out of the surgery and, with her son, Charlie, moved into his house.

When she became pregnant, Kate planned to have an abortion because she felt their relationship was not secure. But Will persuaded her to go ahead with the birth and both were overjoyed with the arrival of Emily in 1997. But happiness turned to heartache when the baby was discovered to be suffering from cystic fibrosis, and the couple moved to Bristol, where a research programme offered some hope of giving the baby a better quality of life.

• Moving back to husband David's native Derbyshire in 1997 with their children, Emma and Tom, Spanish-born Clare – who had met her husband at university and worked as a language teacher – had experienced a nervous breakdown three years earlier. Although that was behind her, she faced new trauma with the onset of manic depression.

Clare was taken into psychiatric care and her condition stabilised after being put on medication. After struggling to find employment, she landed a job at the Brompton Day Centre, helping patients with psychiatric problems.

On becoming pregnant, she had to decide whether to terminate the unborn baby or come off her antidepressants. Choosing to go ahead with the pregnancy, Clare began to show signs of obsessive behaviour but gave birth to a son, William, in the back of a taxi after prematurely going into labour.

NORMAN SHORTHOSE (Clive Swift)

• After running chemist's shops in Derby for 30 years, pompous Norman Shorthose retired to Cardale in 1998 and found that he could not live without work. However, his decision to open a pharmacy was a blow to The Beeches, which had to close its own dispensary, losing the GPs up to 30 per cent of their income.

Surprisingly, hypochondriac Norman was a regular visitor to the surgery and he took a fancy to practice nurse Laura Elliott, but his love was not requited. More seriously, the chemist was approached by The Beeches' locum, Nick Goodson, to connive in a prescription fraud and, later, suffered an angina attack.

LAURA ELLIOTT (Veronica Roberts)

• Vivacious Laura was a divorcée, who left her womanising and alcoholic doctor husband Stuart after 11 years of marriage when her son, Robert – now grown up – was only seven. She joined The Beeches as its practice nurse in 1995, returning to her native Derbyshire from London, and was not fazed by doctors, feeling on a par with them.

Three years later, she left to work for Voluntary Service Overseas, despite the flowers and chocolates brought to her by chemist Norman Shorthose in an attempt to woo her.

1996

A new look was guaranteed to *Peak Practice* for its fourth series, with Simon Shepherd as the only remaining doctor of the original threesome still on screen. Amanda Burton had left to star as a police pathologist in the BBC series *Silent Witness* – turning down a reported £250,000 a year to stay with the ITV programme – and Kevin Whately had filmed a one-off *Inspector Morse* story and Lucy Gannon's BBC 'Screen One' drama *Trip Trap* before seeking new screen roles.

Losing two of its three stars was a challenge for *Peak Practice*'s producers, but Central's parent company, Carlton, marched on with a determination to keep the series among the lynchpins of ITV's weekday evening schedule, this time playing safe with just ten episodes.

Gary Mavers, who had joined as trainee GP Andrew Attwood two-thirds of the way through the previous series, became a permanent fixture on screen. He and Will were joined by Dr Erica Matthews, played by Saskia Wickham, best known for playing the title role in the bodice-ripping *Clarissa* (alongside Sean Bean), as well as Michael Elphick's sidekick, Alex Wilton, in *Boon*.

It was decided to feature four doctors instead of the original line-up of three, and Dr Richard Carey was added to the team, played by Larry Lamb. Frequently seen in a wide variety of character parts on television, Larry had starred as Matt Taylor in the eighties seafaring soap *Triangle* and as Albert Sweet in two series of the sitcom *Get Back*. Larry and Saskia had already played opposite one another in the epic BBC serial *Our Friends in the North* shortly before joining the cast of *Peak Practice*. However, they were destined never to be seen together on screen in the ITV series.

After four episodes had been filmed, Larry and screen wife Jane Wymark were dropped and new producer Richard Handford also left. It was felt that the formula was wrong. As a result, some of the scenes had to be edited or reshot, with Michele Buck resuming control as producer after Jonathan Powell, Carlton's head of drama, who had become the programme's new executive producer, phoned and asked her to return.

'I had always planned to leave after the third series,' says Michele, 'because I foresaw the possibility that there was a huge mountain to climb. Jonathan then phoned and said it was all going horribly wrong and I agreed to look at some tapes of what had been filmed. When I viewed them, I thought that it was a very glossy, good-looking film series, but not *Peak Practice*. I then said I would go back if they did it my way. I analysed the stories and the characters, and I cut Larry out. We had to rewrite and reshoot about nine days' worth of scenes and simply edited him out of other scenes that had already been filmed.

'Larry's character was a former naval surgeon. Although Larry is excellent at what he does, he wasn't a Derbyshire GP. His character, a middle-class, "yo-ho-ho and a bottle of rum" person, didn't bring anything to the story. Suddenly, it was all medical stories and lost its heart. *Peak Practice* has always had a big, golden heart and it lost that.

'Also, because he was posh, Larry's character encroached on Simon's area. So you had a public schoolboy walking round, with whom everyone was very happy, as well as a posh, ex-naval public schoolboy. The show went too "posh", when it was supposed to be about Derbyshire country people.'

Returning to *Peak Practice*, Michele actually saw Kevin Whately and Amanda Burton's departure as an advantage. 'If we hadn't taken those characters out, what would we have done with them?' she asks. 'We invented new characters and, in a funny way, that's when *Peak Practice* really came into its own. There was the possibility that the programme could have been killed when Kevin and Amanda left. But what happened was that it took on a life of its own and the star of the show became the show itself.'

Following the departure of its two biggest stars, and the dramatic exit of one of its new stars, the new-look *Peak Practice* did not die a death, as predicted by some critics, but remained in good health and continued to attract audiences and build up a team of new characters to whom viewers could relate. Another new cast member, James Kerr – previously seen in *Drop the Dead Donkey*, *Just William* and *Prime Suspect 5* – joined as The Beeches' new fund manager, Russ Skinner.

During the series, Will finally found happiness with Dr Kate Webster – actress Shelagh McLeod – who joined the nearby Brompton Health Centre, and Andrew sought to make roots in Cardale at the expense of losing his wife, Kirsty. Erica had a difficult start but, after revealing her personal insecurities, eventually settled in. The seeds were sown for another successful team of television doctors.

Simon Shepherd stayed on as Will to give continuity after Kevin Whately and Amanda Burton's departure, with Gary Mavers returning in his role as Andrew and Saskia Wickham joining the cast as Dr Erica Matthews.

THE CHARACTERS

DR WILL PRESTON (Simon Shepherd)

Now the senior partner after Jack and Beth's decision to stay in Africa, he faces the task of keeping The Beeches afloat and has the confidence to step into a new relationship, with Dr Kate Webster from the health centre.

DR ERICA MATTHEWS (Saskia Wickham)

Following the breakdown of a long-term relationship, city girl Erica joins The Beeches as a locum after six years of working in a Manchester practice. After a difficult beginning, she settles in and wins the respect and affection of colleagues and patients.

DR ANDREW ATTWOOD (Gary Mavers)

Having spent several months as a trainee at The Beeches, where his duties included running the antenatal clinic, Andrew has to decide whether to stay or return to his native Liverpool and wife Kirsty.

DR KATE WEBSTER (Shelagh McLeod)

After turning down Will's offer of a partnership at The Beeches in favour of the rival Brompton Health Centre, Kate falls for Will's charms. She, too, is divorced and has a young son the same age as Will's.

KIRSTY ATTWOOD (Sukie Smith)

Andrew's wife, Kirsty – who supported her husband financially while he attended medical school – is under pressure to leave Liverpool and join him in the Peak District, but hopes to stay put and train as a teacher.

RUSS SKINNER (James Kerr)

Following Trevor Sharp's departure as fund manager at The Beeches, Russ Skinner leaves his job at the Family Health Service Authority to take over.

KIM BEARDSMORE (Esther Coles)

Still on the lookout for romance, practice manager Kim's reunion with old school friend Alec Kitson has come to nothing.

LAURA ELLIOTT (Veronica Roberts)

Practice nurse Laura continues to dispense wise advice – to patients and doctors.

JAMES and CHLOE WHITE (Richard Platt and Hazel Ellerby)

Pub landlords James and Chloë, whose first attempt at fostering was with an eight-year-old called Matthew, take in teenager Gary Simms.

ALICE NORTH (Margery Mason)

Cardale OAP Alice has persuaded Will Shepherd to stay in the village instead of taking up a new job as medical adviser to the North Riding Health Authority.

LEFT *Saskia Wickham joined* Peak Practice *as Dr Erica Matthews after leading television roles in* Clarissa, Boon *and* Our Friends in the North, *following the departure of Amanda Burton.*

WILL KEEPS THE BEECHES AFLOAT

Will was left holding The Beeches together when Beth and Jack left for Africa. They had intially gone on sabbatical leave, but later changed their mind, and decided to stay, buying into the Johannesburg clinic where they had both been working.

With fund manager Trevor Sharp gone as well, the practice's staff were begining to look a little thin on the ground. Then, following a decline in patient numbers, the Family Health Service Authority (FHSA) instructed Will that The Beeches should become a two-partner practice and warned him to install a fund manager within a month, otherwise fundholder status would be reconsidered.

Taking the bit between his teeth, Will poached FHSA financial consultant Russ Skinner to take up the position of fund manager and arranged for Andrew Attwood and Erica Matthews, who had recently joined them, to remain as locums.

ERICA'S JITTERY START

During her early days at The Beeches, before becoming a partner, Erica found the workload exhausting and rued the day she had arrived. She couldn't wait to finish her contract and beat a hasty retreat.

One day, while searching for a house in a remote part of the Peaks and becoming frustrated with the speed of the van in front of her car, she overtook it and assumed she was to blame when she next saw the vehicle in a river. On turning back to help, she was horrified to discover eight-year-old Debbie Priest trapped inside the submerged van driven by her father, Mick.

Erica dived into the water and hauled the unconscious girl to safety. An ambulance was called and Debbie was taken to hospital, where she underwent an operation for a ruptured spleen. Eventually, she came out of her coma and made a steady recovery.

Guilt turned to shock when Erica learnt that Mick Priest had been suffering from blackouts and a scan revealed that he was suffering from a brain tumour. Both Erica and Mick's wife, Cathy, were furious that he had endangered

- **Saskia Wickham** was thrown in at the deep end right from her first few scenes in *Peak Practice*. As Erica Matthews, she had to plunge into icy water to save eight-year-old Debbie Priest, whose father's van was submerged in a river.

For most of the shots showing her in the water, Saskia was filmed in an outdoor swimming pool. She was also filmed at a river, although stuntwoman **Sarah Franzl** – who later doubled for Kate Winslet in the film *Titanic* – stood in for some of the shots. **Kieron Shah**, a 4ft 2in Indian

both his and his daughter's life rather than face up to his illness. Mick was terrified of the surgery – there was a chance that he might be left paralysed as a result – but he was talked round by Will. The operation was a total success.

Erica gradually adjusted to life in the Peaks and put her roots down in Cardale, a very different environment to the Manchester inner-city practice where she had worked previously.

stunt actor who has appeared in films such as *Superman* and *Star Wars*, doubled for the child actress, **Victoria Betterton**, in the underwater scenes.

Stunt co-ordinator **Roy Alon**, who acted as second-unit director for the scene, recalls: 'We required a scene of the child being pulled out of the car and emerging from the water, so we did that in a swimming pool under the most controlled and safe environment.

'To re-create the river scene filmed earlier, Saskia jumped in, opened the van door and pulled out Kieron, the child's stunt double. We were able to film that in close-up. Saskia had also done some scenes at the river, supervised by me and her stunt double. It was bloody freezing, but she was excellent and gave us very good value.'

In the story, the child's father, Mick Priest, was played by **David Michaels**, who had already acted hairdresser Jon Welch in *Coronation Street* and went on to take the role of Dr Neil Bolton in *Heartbeat*. **Denise Stephenson**, previously seen as Chief Supt Don Henderson's wife in the Phil Redmond BBC police series *Waterfront Beat*, acted the girl's mother, Cathy.

After rescuing eight-year-old Debbie Priest (Victoria Betterton) from the submerged van driven by her father, Mick (David Michaels), Erica administers the kiss of life.

NOT SUCH A FUN RUN FOR MADDIE

The Cardale Fun Run was held to raise money to buy medical equipment for The Beeches. One of the participants, Maddie Taylor, 15-year-old diabetic daughter of the village's widowed police sergeant, Dave Taylor, collapsed later at home. Andrew, who had been treating her diabetes, assumed that the teenager had suffered a hypoglycaemic attack – low blood sugar – only to discover that the teenager was three months pregnant.

Maddie broke the news to her 18-year-old boyfriend, Ewan Harvey, then told her father, who exploded and insisted that she have an abortion. Dave was further incensed on discovering that Andrew had arranged for his daughter to visit a teenage mothers' centre in Derby to allow Maddie to make a more informed decision. As a result, she was determined to keep the baby.

Dave lodged a complaint at The Beeches and sought the advice of his close friend, practice nurse Laura Elliott. He also told Maddie that she could not stay under his roof if she had the baby. Maddie walked out and went to stay with Ewan, who began to have doubts about keeping the baby. It finally became too much for Maddie when even Andrew appeared to back-pedal about having the baby on her own. His wife, Kirsty, had made him see that his decision to support Maddie's right not to have an abortion might have been linked to Kirsty's own termination 13 years earlier.

Maddie packed her belongings and took off into the High Peaks to allow the situation to cool down. In her rush to escape, she forgot her food and suffered a hypoglycaemic attack on the mountain. When a rescue team started to search in the wrong place, Ewan realised that she would have gone to Devil's Reach and raced ahead with Andrew. Maddie was found just before dawn and Andrew remained with her while Ewan went for help.

When assistance arrived later that morning, both Maddie and Andrew were suffering from hypothermia and were rushed to hospital. The rescue brought reconciliation with it. Dave agreed to Maddie having the baby, and he also made friends with Ewan and agreed to give him the chance to look after his child.

- **Paul Moriarty**, who had played Sgt Bill Wells in *A Touch of Frost* before taking the role of George Palmer in *EastEnders*, acted widowed police sergeant Dave Taylor, who brought his 15-year-old daughter, Maddie, up strictly. Maddie was acted by **Sarah-Jane Potts**, who has since acted Harriet Potter in *The Broker's Man*, Alice Pierce in *The Locksmith* and Virginia Otis in *The Canterville Ghost*. Maddie's boyfriend, Ewan Harvey, was played by **Jonathan Kerrigan**, who subsequently joined *Casualty* as Sam Colloby.

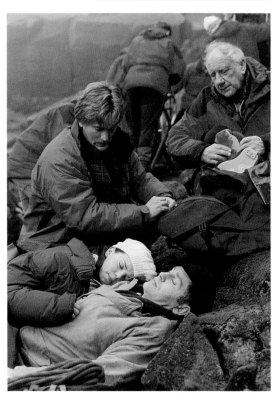

Will and a rescue team arrive to find diabetic Maddie Taylor (Sarah-Jane Potts) and Andrew suffering from hypothermia after a night in the High Peaks.

DOCTOR ENDS HIS OWN LIFE

Recently widowed Dr Philip Ramsden had run his one-man High Peaks surgery for years. Nearing retirement and suffering from the early stages of Alzheimer's disease, he provided patient care to the remote villages in the Peaks and – after being told by the FHSA that his surgery would not remain viable – he worried what would happen to his patients when it eventually closed.

When Jill Bentley, who was expecting her first baby, collapsed in Cardale after suffering a dizzy spell, Erica was appalled to find that Dr Ramsden had prescribed her medication that was unsuitable for a pregnant woman.

Andrew was later called out to Dr Ramsden when he accidentally cut his hand while slicing a loaf of bread. Will advised the doctor that it was time to retire with dignity for his patients' sake and warned him that, if he failed to do so, he would have no choice but to report him to the FHSA.

Will carried out his threat and a doctor from the FHSA paid him a visit, with the result that Dr Ramsden handed in his resignation. He visited Will at The Beeches to confess his fear of Alzheimer's disease and requested that Will take on some of his patients. Unable to face up to a lonely and frightening future, Dr Ramsden returned home and took a fatal drugs overdose.

Meanwhile, Jill went into premature labour and managed to get to The Beeches in a taxicab. The baby was delivered by the doctors and nurse Laura. News of the birth was phoned through to Dr Ramsden's surgery as secretary Emma Davies returned from an errand in Nottingham to find her boss dead, slumped over his desk.

• Veteran Lancashire-born actor **Glyn Owen**, who acted ailing High Peaks' GP Dr Philip Ramsden, is best known for his television roles as Irish casualty officer Patrick O'Meara in *Emergency – Ward 10*, Richard Hurst in the spy series *The Rat Catchers*, Norman Lindley in *Coronation Street*, Edward Hammond in *The Brothers* and Jack Rolfe in *Howards' Way*.

Dr Philip Ramsden (Glyn Owen), suffering the first stages of Alzheimer's disease, faces up to the closure of his High Peaks' surgery.

WILL FINDS A NEW HOME...

Will had done with skulking in his bachelor pad and bought a beautiful Georgian house for himself on the edge of Cardale. Everything seemed rosier as the wounds of his divorce finally began to heal and he looked forward to the future.

But Will was temporarily knocked off balance when ex-wife Sarah arrived to give him four weeks' notice that she and her new boyfriend would be taking sons Tony and Julian to live with them in Florida. Will was angry and upset at losing his sons, but he accepted that they all had to put the past behind them and that it was time to get on with their lives. He gave Sarah his blessing and enjoyed a last weekend with the boys before they emigrated.

...AND A NEW WOMAN

When Erica became Will's tenant in the cottage adjoining his house, she tried to contain the crush she had on her eligible boss. But any designs that she had on Will fell by the wayside when he brought Dr Kate Webster to Erica's housewarming party. It became obvious to everyone that Will had eyes only for the striking woman doctor with a mane of chestnut hair.

The two doctors had a lot in common. They were both partners in a medical practice and had both gone through disastrous marriages. Kate also had a son, Charlie, who was away at boarding school near Matlock. When Will took Kate on a surprise date to the opera, he realised that he had finally met a woman after his own heart when they both opted to leave the performance because they were so bored. He presumed that, because Sarah had liked

that sort of entertainment, all women would. Kate was clearly not all women and, when they went back to Will's house, they quickly fell into bed.

Kate eventually gave in to Will's persistent requests that she move into his house. He was knocked for six when Kate announced that she was pregnant, but that she planned to have an abortion because she felt their relationship lacked stability.

Will asked Kate to keep the baby and marry him, much to her disbelief, given that they had both only recently come out of messy divorces. However, she eventually relented and agreed to have the baby. Both Kate and Will felt they would like to give their relationship a go and stay together to raise their child, although Kate felt it was far too soon to think about marriage.

Will finally finds happiness with Dr Kate Webster (Shelagh McLeod) after the turmoil of his marriage break-up and his fling with drugs rep Janey Cooper.

BROTHER IN LAW-BREAKING

Following their experience of fostering Matthew, James and Chloë White took in 14-year-old Gary Simms, although he was very unhappy at The Manor Hotel. Then Gary's 17-year-old brother, Lee, hitched a lift into Cardale with Erica and Will. Afterwards, Will discovered that Lee had helped himself to a £25 bottle of malt whisky from the back of his Range Rover.

Will was surprised to find Lee at The Beeches the next day. Laura had brought him in from the roadside for a shower, some breakfast and a checkup for his nasty cough. Will examined Lee and sent him on his way with a prescription for antibiotics. Arriving at The Manor Hotel, Lee asked Gary to run away to Scarborough with him.

Concerned that Lee was coughing up blood, a worried Gary made an anonymous phone call to The Beeches about his brother's chest problems. After Erica persuaded Lee to visit her at The Beeches, where she took a sputum sample, he picked up the charity collection box on his way out.

Returning to the barn that he had been sleeping in, Lee discovered the farmer had burned all his belongings. Convinced that the farmer had been tipped off by The Beeches, he lobbed a brick through the surgery window, narrowly missing Erica.

It emerged that Lee was on the run from a detention centre where he had been held for breaking and entering. Erica offered Lee a temporary home at her cottage, but her old love Dan Copeland – trying to worm his way back into Erica's affections – led him to believe that Erica had informed on him to the police.

Terrified of being locked up again, Lee fled Cardale with Gary in tow just as Erica received his test results, which revealed that he was suffering from TB. Will, Erica and Chloë gave chase, finally catching up with Lee and Gary at Derby Bus Station. Gary was reconciled with Chloë and taken back to The Manor Hotel, while Lee went to hospital for treatment.

ERICA PUTS 'EILEEN' TO REST

When Erica was asked by elderly eccentric Edward Fellows to pay a home visit to 'Eileen', she discovered that the woman was no more than an imaginary companion – constantly ill and becoming quite a burden to him.

Erica decided to free Edward by telling him that Eileen had died. This seemed to do the trick and, only days later, Edward turned up at The Beeches with a bunch of flowers for Erica and told that her that he was getting out and about more.

> • Eccentric Edward Fellows, whose imaginary companion 'Eileen' was declared dead by Erica, was played by veteran comedy actor **Ken Jones**. He played Leslie Mills in *Her Majesty's Pleasure*, Rex in *The Squirrels*, Billy Clarkson in *The Wackers*, Ives in *Porridge*, Det. Sgt Arnold Nixon in *The Nesbitts Are Coming*, Dave Locket in *Seconds Out*, Archangel Derek in *Dead Earnest* and Uncle Bernard in *Watching*.

BRUISED IN BODY AND MIND

Twelve-year-old Stuart Reynolds stayed with father Barry, a fish farmer, when mother Angela ran off with her husband's business partner, Malcolm. When Angela started a bitter custody battle, Stuart – who suffered from dyspraxia, a condition of physical disco-ordination – pleaded to remain with Barry and grumbled at having to visit his mother and Malcom.

Andrew was called to examine Stuart at the local police station after the boy had fallen and hurt his wrist whilst clambering on a car parked at The Manor Hotel. When he noticed severe bruising to the boy's back, he suspected physical abuse. Will, Barry's friend and squash partner, asked Barry about the suspected abuse, believing that Malcolm might be to blame. Barry denied there was a problem, but that night Andrew and wife Kirsty saw him laying into Stuart in the street. As they tried to intervene, Barry dragged the boy to his car and drove off, telling them to mind their own business.

Will discovered horrific bruises on Stuart's body and confronted Barry, who admitted to hitting his son. Seeing that Barry was unable to cope with the stress of the custody battle, he decided not to do anything until after the hearing. But Andrew, believing Stuart to be in danger, lodged a report with social services that was read out in court. As a result, Angela won custody, with Barry getting supervised contact at a special contact centre. Stuart was heartbroken, but his father reassured him that Angela did love him and that he would be fine in her care.

Facing the stress of a custody battle, Barry Reynolds (Greg Hicks) physically abuses son Stuart (James Tomlinson).

OAP IN WHEEL DANGER

Elderly Fred Hargrave's driving was rather like his beat-up old car – well past its sell-by date. Oblivious to other road users, Fred ran practice nurse Laura off the road, but, thanks to her quick reactions, a nasty accident was avoided.

Laura, who suffered whiplash injuries in the incident, couldn't believe her eyes when Fred, with his much beleaguered wife, Rose, in tow, drove up to The Beeches; he'd come to see someone about his back pain. She eventually managed to make Fred see that it was time for him to hang up his driving gloves and to let Rose take the wheel in future.

• Another veteran actor, **Derek Benfield**, who took the role of doddery driver Fred Hargrave, played three roles in *Coronation Street* in the sixties. More recently, he has guest-starred in many series and acted Patricia Routledge's long-suffering screen husband, Robert, in *Hetty Wainthropp Investigates.*

ERICA BECOMES A PARTNER

Dr Kate Webster had rejected Will's offer of a partnership in favour of one at the Brompton Health Centre, following the departure of Dr John Reginald.

Will, assuming that Erica and Andrew were not interested in permanent jobs in Cardale, decided to advertise for a suitable partner without consulting them, much to their annoyance. Discovering his mistake, Will apologised, and they both applied for the partnership, but Andrew failed to make it through to the interview stage after Will informed him that The Beeches needed a woman. Andrew was hurt and felt discriminated against. He pointed out that he had been running the antenatal clinic with no problems.

Erica was offered a partnership while Andrew was left to lick his wounds. Then a revised decision

Kirsty Attwood (Sukie Smith) is reluctant to stay in Cardale with husband Andrew and wants to return home to Liverpool.

from the FHSA stated that The Beeches could remain a three-partner practice after all, since the surgery had taken over the late Dr Philip Ramsden's High Peaks patient list. Will immediately offered a partnership to Andrew, who tried to persuade his wife, Kirsty, that the green fields of Cardale held a rosier future for them than Liverpool.

But Kirsty felt that Andrew was being selfish and only considering himself. She had worked to support him when he was at medical school and now she felt it was her turn. Unlike Andrew, she did not want to start a family yet because she wanted to train as a teacher. Kirsty thought that living in the country would hinder her opportunities. As Will kept the partnership offer on hold, Kirsty returned to Liverpool to think the situation over.

ERICA'S PERSONAL QUEST

Events were a little too close to home for Erica when she became involved with the care of 20-year-old Chris Curtis, Will's kidney dialysis patient. When Chris, who lived with his parents and was doing a distance learning course, became ill with an infected fistula – a dialysis access point artificially constructed from a union of veins – he was told that his only hope was to have a transplant operation.

Chris had a rare tissue match and, with no suitable donors available, his only hope was for a kidney from either of his parents, Clare or Tom. But a weeping Clare dropped the bombshell that neither she nor Tom were Chris's natural parents. The couple had never told their son that he was adopted, and he was now so devastated by the news that he refused to speak to them.

With Chris's permission, Erica sought and

found his biological mother, Helen Marsh, who was now married with a family of her own – but in trying to browbeat Helen into helping, Erica failed to get her co-operation.

Facing Will's wrath, Erica wept as she told him that getting Chris's real mother to help was as much about proving to herself that her natural mother would do the same for her. Will had not realised that Erica was adopted and his heart went out to her. As Erica went back to apologise to Helen, Chris's real mother had a change of heart and agreed to donate a kidney if their organs were compatible. Chris was then reconciled with Clare and Tom before his successful transplant operation.

ERICA STRUGGLES WITH INSECURITY

Erica admitted to Will that she had allowed her emotions to colour her judgement when dealing with Chris Curtis, the kidney transplant patient who needed to trace his natural parents. She sought affection and, as a result, this sometimes laid her open to being hurt.

Her crush on Will had come to nothing when he fell in love with Kate Webster. However, when her old love Dan Copeland from Manchester turned up in Cardale wanting to pick up where they had left off, she realised that their relationship had reached a dead end and gave him his marching orders.

Andrew's break-up with wife Kirsty brought him closer to Erica, who had enjoyed a good friendship with Kirsty. On returning from a trip to Liverpool in an attempt to salvage his marriage, Andrew went for supper with Erica and ended up in

Erica embraces former love Dan Copeland (Edward Atterton) when he arrives from Manchester, but she realises theirs is a dead-end relationship.

bed with her. The following morning, Andrew was filled with guilt and remorse – he was a married man and Kirsty was the only woman with whom he had ever slept.

A SNIP TOO LATE

When Cardale superdad Harry Fielding decided that he and his wife, Tricia, had enough with five children in their family, he requested a vasectomy. Once Andrew had reassured Tricia that her husband's sexual performance would not be affected, she gave her permission for Will to carry out the operation under a local anaesthetic at The Beeches.

However, the operation proved to be a case of 'closing the stable door after the horse had bolted' when the Fielding family arrived back at the surgery only days later to announce that Tricia was already pregnant with their sixth child.

• Real medical attention was needed when guest star **Billy Geraghty** came a cropper after filming his role as vasectomy patient Harry Fielding. When producer Michele Buck needed to re-shoot some of his scenes after Larry Lamb was dropped from the cast as Dr Richard Carey, she found that Billy had broken his collarbone and it would be three months before he could work again.

Billy, who starred as Buddy Holly in the West End musical *Buddy*, has also appeared in series such as *Heartbeat*, *The Bill*, *Soldier Soldier*, *The Riff Raff Element* and *Backup*, as well as playing Cliff in the London-only ITV serial *London Bridge*.

MANAGERS GET IT TOGETHER

The Beeches practice manager, Kim Beardsmore, was involved in a budding romance with fund manager Russ Skinner. He took her out for a meal in the evening to The Manor Hotel, but left her high and dry when he dashed away clutching his chest, leaving Kim upset and embarrassed.

The reason for Russ's hasty exit eventually came to light after he collapsed with chest pains at an FHSA dinner dance. He was suffering from an overdose of caffeine after consuming about 20 cups of coffee a day. When Kim was told of Russ's plight, she forgave him and the two looked forward to another date.

A CHANGE OF MIND

When Andrew discovered that Roy Bennet, who lived with daughter Julie Evans and grandson Neil, was suffering from liver cancer, alarm bells rang for the young doctor, who suspected that the cancer might have been caused by the carcinogenic material that Roy had come into contact with for years in a plastics factory. Roy felt it was too late to do anything about it and, after being warned by a surgeon that an operation was very risky, turned one down in favour of enjoying what life he had left.

Andrew pleaded with Julie to change her father's mind, which she did, although Roy insisted he was going ahead with the operation simply for his daughter's sake. When the operation was a success, Andrew dashed down to join Roy and his family in their bedside celebrations at the hospital. However, their happiness was short-lived when Roy died shortly afterwards from a pulmonary embolism, a fatal lung complication.

• **Mark Kingston**, another prolific character actor whose many TV roles include Geoff in the Penelope Keith sitcom *No Job for a Lady*, acted liver cancer victim Roy Bennet. His daughter, Julie Evans, was played by **Gillian Bevan**, hot from her role as Det. Supt Rose Penfold in one series of *The Chief*. She has since been seen as Ruth in the sitcom *Loved by You*.

DRIVEN TO VIOLENCE

Cab driver Des Manningham, a recovering alcoholic and former soldier, was fiercely protective of his wife, Linda, who suffered from multiple sclerosis (MS). When Des brought her to The Beeches suffering the injuries of yet

• Multiple sclerosis sufferer Linda Manningham was played by **Judy Flynn**, best known as daft secretary Julie

another fall, Will explained that her MS had reached its secondary degenerative phase, and that her periods of remission were over.

While Linda accepted the news and tried to deal with the impact it would have on her life, Des did not and accused Will of incompetence. Visiting the Brompton Health Centre, he believed that Dr Kate Webster would be able to do more for Linda. When Kate suggested that he contact the Multiple Sclerosis Society, Des misunderstood and thought it would be able to offer him a cure for Linda.

On phoning the society, Des realised that MS had no miracle cure and he snapped. He lashed out at Kate, knocking her to the floor of her office and leaving her with a face full of bruises. She called the police and Des was arrested. On hearing the news, Will risked being struck off as a doctor by knocking Des through a plate glass door.

The Manninghams then fell in arrears with their mortgage and received a threat to repossess their house. Kate agreed to drop her complaint about Des to the police and persuaded their building society manager to come to an arrangement over the arrears. With the financial pressure behind them, and Des finally able to accept Linda's MS, the future looked brighter for the Manninghams.

in six series of *The Brittas Empire* and Madge Althorpe in *The House of Eliott*.

'It's a big responsibility to portray a condition like MS in a believable way in a TV programme,' she says. 'But I was helped enormously by a woman sufferer from Derby, who bravely came to the set to talk to me about it.

'She had only been diagnosed for three months but was really open and honest. I'd got a couple of medical books out from my local library, but it wasn't until I met this lady that I started to understand what MS means for both the sufferer and their family.'

Lawrence Mullin played the building society manager who agreed a method for Linda and her husband to pay their mortgage arrears. He was previously seen as Carl Edwards in the BBC series *Degrees of Error*, and is still remembered as Mike Baldwin's factory van driver Steve Fisher in *Coronation Street* in the seventies and as 'a very, very nice man' in an AA commercial.

DOCTOR-PATIENT RELATIONS

Andrew was at rock bottom and on antidepressants when he struck up a friendship with first-year medical student Louise Siddons. The pair had met when Andrew visited her father, Patrick, a former naval commander, who had suffered a series of falls.

• Former naval commander Patrick Siddons, who burned himself after stumbling into his Aga, was played by **Edward Hardwicke**, son of film and stage legend Sir Cedric Hardwicke. Edward acted escape officer Pat Grant in the seventies series *Colditz* and took over the role of Dr Watson in ITV's Sherlock Holmes dramas alongside Jeremy Brett in 1985, when actor David Burke left after two series.

Andrew winds up in trouble after rejecting the advances of medical student Louise Siddons (Lucy Tregear), who then accuses him of assaulting her.

As a child, Edward harboured ambitions of becoming a doctor, but he began following in the family tradition at the age of eight, when he appeared in the war-time Spencer Tracy film *A Guy Named Joe.*

The GP saw his relationship with Louise as a crutch, one where they propped each other up and offered each other a caring ear. But to Louise it was much more. She visited Andrew at The Beeches with a throat infection and tried to kiss him, but fled hurt and humiliated from the surgery after an embarrassed Andrew pulled away and told her that she had misread the situation.

When Louise told her father that Andrew had 'touched' her, Patrick lodged an official complaint. Eventually, Louise broke down in front of Erica one evening and told her the truth. Louise felt that she could not cope with anything any more – she hated studying medicine and had failed all her first-year tests.

Andrew breathed a sigh of relief when the complaint against him was dropped, Louise agreed to go for counselling and Patrick finally allowed Erica to arrange for treatment of his glaucoma, an eye disease.

HEART-STOPPING BIRTHDAY

Sarah-Jane White's fourth birthday party nearly ended in tragedy when Chloë and James's only child developed a lethal infection after falling and knocking one of her teeth out. The accident triggered endocarditis, a bacterial infection that had affected the functioning of a heart valve.

Hospital tests showed that a congenital heart defect had allowed the infection to take hold.

Chloë maintained a round-the-clock bedside vigil as James ran himself ragged trying to cope with running The Manor Hotel singlehanded. Surgeons told the couple that Sarah-Jane had the beginnings of heart failure and would need an operation to repair

the damaged valve, but Chloë refused to give her permission. She considered the risks involved to be too great.

When James could bear the situation no longer, he gave the go-ahead for the operation without Chloë's knowledge and returned to The Manor Hotel rather than face a tongue-lashing from his wife. But the couple were reunited when Will called James back to the hospital, saying that Chloë needed him. The couple were

• When James and Chloë White's daughter, Sarah-Jane, faced heart surgery, **Art Malik** played surgeon Mr Singh. He is still best remembered as tragic Hari Kumar in ITV's epic series *The Jewel in the Crown*, but he has also appeared in mini-series such as *The Far Pavilions*, *The Wimbledon Poisoner* and *Turning World*, as well as the films *The Living Daylights* and *City of Joy*.

relieved when Sarah-Jane's operation went successfully and the damaged heart valve was repaired.

ANDREW BURNS HIS BRIDGES

When estranged wife Kirsty returned to give Andrew her support over Louise Siddons's complaint against him, the couple agreed to give their marriage another chance – in Liverpool. But, as they made their way to Andrew's leaving party at The Beeches, Kirsty plucked up the courage to point out that they had drifted apart and that it was too late to save their 13-year-old marriage. She returned to Liverpool alone and Andrew arrived, brokenhearted, at his party and announced that he would be staying.

GARY MAVERS
as Dr Andrew Attwood

To millions of adoring female fans, Gary Mavers as *Peak Practice* GP Dr Andrew Attwood is just what the doctor ordered – blond, sexy and with a wonderful bedside manner. The Liverpudlian actor seems to wear the heart-throb label almost as well as his sixties-style clothes and manages to take all the adulation in his stride.

Luckily for him, so does his wife, Sue, a freelance make-up artist. 'Sue's in the business and knows the way it all works,' he explains. 'She knew me long before all this

happened and she's cool about it.'

A good job, too, because according to Gary she often gets pushed out of the way when his fans make a beeline for him. 'It's as if they don't see her,' he says. 'It's a lack of consideration for her and all manners go out of the window and I kind of resent it.'

But, overall, Gary is thrilled that *Peak Practice* turned him into a star, and claims that Andrew is as much like himself as he could possibly make him. 'I put my personality into the character and the writers just went from there,' he says. 'They had originally wanted my character to come from Sheffield or Leeds but, after meeting me a couple of times, decided that I should use my native accent, which is much more interesting.'

Peak Practice gave the RADA-trained actor a chance to stretch his range in a string of challenging storylines, such as the explosive crash scene in which Andrew suffered a collapsed lung. Gary recalls long hours filming in temperatures of six degrees below zero. 'I was only wearing a thin suit, which had to be ripped,' he says, 'so I wasn't allowed to wear any thermals.

'We filmed from five in the evening until five the next morning. It was hard work and there was nowhere to shelter from the cold. There was me, a 72-year-old actor and another, young actor, and we basically had our bollocks frozen off!'

Peak Practice also brought Gary together on screen with daughter Abby, his child from a past relationship. Like any father, Gary is immensely proud of her and says he was delighted when casting director Julia Lisney called him to ask whether Abby would like the part of the daughter of Andrew's Liverpudlian friend, Phil Young. 'I've never been a pushy parent who wants their child to be an actor. In fact, I wouldn't encourage her. It's hard enough for actors to make it, but for women it seems there are half as many parts and twice as many actresses, so it's really depressing. But it was nice to work with her as it gave her the chance to see what Dad does when he's away.'

The series has also enabled Gary to indulge his love of clothes. 'Andrew has my kind of look,' says Gary. 'His stuff is the sort that I wear in real life. I think his clothes are classy, look good and I feel comfortable in them.' But, although they are stylish, Gary insists they don't make him look like a fashion victim. 'They are understated rather than being out-and-out designer gear,' he explains. 'The last thing you want is to upstage the character by his clothes – you've got to blend in.'

Gary is also a self-confessed car freak who owns a 1963 Mercedes sports convertible, which he lovingly restored. And, although he likes Andrew's classic red Volvo, he feels the character should have moved on to another model. 'When we chose the car for Andrew he was a struggling, young, trainee GP,' he says. 'But he should be able to afford something better now he has a few bob in the bank.'

For Gary, *Peak Practice* is a wonderful learning experience. 'Other work I have done was over in six weeks or so, but *Peak Practice* films for eight or nine months of the year,' he says. 'Things are constantly changing, there are different directors, cameramen, alternate crew, and visiting artists. These factors make sure you're constantly kept on your toes.'

Gary was previously seen on television as the handsome mill foreman Hal in the television series *Body & Soul*, providing Kristin Scott Thomas with a shoulder to cry on. He had made his screen début in the television film *The Man From the Pru*, starring Jonathan Pryce, Susannah York and Anna Massey. 'It was great,' he recalls. 'I couldn't have wished for a better first television part, working with people of such a high calibre.' Before filming the sixth series of *Peak Practice*, Gary shot his starring role in *The Unknown Soldier*, a three-part, First World War romantic drama in which he portrayed a shell-shocked soldier.

Ultimately, Gary wants to make it in film. 'I think as an actor you get to a point in television when you can't go any further and the next step is films,' he says.

SASKIA WICKHAM
as Dr Erica Matthews

The on-screen sexual chemistry between Saskia Wickham and Gary Mavers was so powerful that the actress believes they became a modern-day Spencer Tracy and Katharine Hepburn. 'Not that I put myself in the same class,' she adds, 'but there are some people where there is a certain frisson, and it is there with me and Gary.

'I loved doing scenes with him, but funnily enough they weren't going to get us together at all in the programme until they noticed that there was something exciting between us.'

It all seems so cosy, but how did the actors' real-life partners react to their sexual sparring on television? Fear not. Saskia – who left *Peak Practice* at the end of the sixth series after Erica jilted Gary on their wedding day – says that there was never any awkwardness. 'Gary knows my boyfriend and I know his wife, Sue, terribly well,' she says. 'It was just a really easy situation, despite my boyfriend's joke that I spent more time in bed with Gary than I did with him.'

Saskia confesses to being sad that Erica

and Andrew didn't make it to the altar after all. 'She must have been crazy,' says the actress. 'I looked at Andrew in his wedding outfit and I thought: "Why won't she marry you?" The problem was that Erica was quite a self-destructive person and would always stop herself from being happy. I think she had a lot of baggage to sort out about her natural parents.'

Joining *Peak Practice* after starring in *Boon* as Michael Elphick's leather-clad secretary, Alex, Saskia enjoyed watching the character of Erica grow. 'In the beginning, Erica was always trying to smooth the waters,' she says. 'Then, without losing any of her impetuousness, she became more central, although she could still fly off the handle now and again, which I loved.'

Always up for a challenge, Saskia found one of the most difficult episodes in *Peak Practice* in her first scene – underwater. 'The whole thing was quite frightening and most of it was done with me wearing weights underwater in a swimming pool,' she explains. 'After the first take, someone forgot to remove the weights and, as I sank steadily to the bottom of the pool, I thought: "Oh, dear, the end of my career – and my life!"'

Having not watched *Peak Practice* before landing the part of Erica, she joined with no preconceptions and qualms about following in the footsteps of Amanda Burton. 'One of the strengths of the show is that it can bring new people in,' she says. 'I'm not in the same slot as Amanda. It was a very different character, so I just found it very exciting.'

To get the feel of the programme, Saskia talked to her brother Caspar's wife, Jo, who is a doctor. 'As a woman, it interests me how she copes with dramatic situations in everyday life,' says Saskia. 'It was useful to get into the psyche of a person rather than just finding out the medical nitty-gritty.'

One of the perks of working on *Peak Practice* was Erica's lovely clothes. Saskia herself is a self-confessed clothes fiend, and she relished wearing some of the character's designer gear. 'I went shopping with the costume designer to choose Erica's clothes,' she says. 'Obviously, you can't just have the things that you would like but, if it does so happen that she likes a little Donna Karan or Ralph Lauren number, what can I do about it? I've a terrible taste for expensive clothes.'

Over three series, Saskia – who was also delighted to welcome her actor parents, Jeffrey Wickham and Clair Stewart, to *Peak Practice* when they appeared as her adoptive parents – found many elements of her screen character that she admired. 'I would like to be as clever, forthright, impulsive and daring as she is,' says Saskia. 'Creating a character really is like creating a fantasy of yourself.'

Another part that Saskia enjoyed playing since leaving the Central School of Speech and Drama was the title role in the BBC's costume drama *Clarissa*, alongside Sean Bean. 'Working on *Clarissa* was amazing,' she recalls. 'I don't think I have ever had such a fantastic time. It was all like a magical mystery tour as we filmed at Ealing Studios. I remember sitting in Dressing Room One, where all those legendary Ealing comedy stars had sat, and I was totally gobsmacked.'

Saskia, who made her professional début in the children's drama *The Villains* at the age of eight, says that her favourite medium is definitely television. 'It is made for real people,' she says. 'I want to entertain people and I think television is where it is at – the creative cutting edge, I feel.'

ADRIAN LUKIS
as Dr David Shearer

Playing flawed characters is one of Adrian Lukis's greatest loves. When he landed his role as Dr David Shearer in *Peak Practice*, he had the chance to scratch beneath the surface to find out what really made this country GP tick. 'My notion is that he is someone who needs to be there all the time for everybody,' says Adrian. 'He tries very hard to be a good doctor, husband and father, but there is something beneath the drive to be perfect.'

After a string of classical roles on stage with the Royal Shakespeare Company, and the part of Wickham in the BBC serial Jane Austen's *Pride and Prejudice*, the actor saw the chance to make his mark on television in a long-running role. 'I thought it would be a good thing thing to do something on popular television and a wonderful chance to actually tackle a role and stamp my authority on it,' he says.

One particular aspect that Adrian has enjoyed about working on *Peak Practice* was the chance to work with so many of the guest stars. 'They are such fun people,' he says, with a smile. 'We go out and have a grand old time, particularly Caroline Berry, who is an old friend of mine, and Tom Lockyer, who played the scabby doctor who was doing everyone down.' Adrian also enjoyed being teamed with his screen wife, Fiona Gillies. 'Working with her is a complete joy – she's lovely and we get on very well. She's funny and bright, and we laugh a lot.'

Appearing in *Peak Practice* also helped Adrian to overcome his inhibition in front of the camera. 'Because working in television leaves no time for a big method number,' he says, 'it is very personality-based and it has taught me to be much more relaxed when filming.'

Adrian was happy to be eased into *Peak Practice* in the 1997 series when Simon Shepherd stayed on for the first four episodes to give continuity after Kevin Whately and Amanda Burton's departure. This, Adrian believes, prevented the viewers from suffering withdrawal symptoms when all three of the original doctors left. He then moved in to tackle his role, changing some of the character's stereotyping as he went along.

'There was a danger in the beginning for us to think that, because he was a 40-year-old doctor, he should be all big sweaters and Barbours and sit around listening to light classical music,' says Adrian. 'But I think David has evolved and grown stronger. He's had his hair cut shorter and his clothes have loosened up. After all, I don't want to play him as an old fogey.'

Before acting baddy Wickham in the BBC adaptation of Jane Austen's *Pride and Prejudice*, Adrian made occasional screen appearances in programmes such as *The Bretts*, Granada Television's *Sherlock Holmes* series and *Prime Suspect*.

But Adrian's first love is theatre, particularly playing Shakespeare. 'I've done a couple of stints at the Royal Shakespeare Company and I'd like to go back and play Richard II, Macbeth and Hamlet,' he says. 'There is something about Shakespeare which is so fantastic to do.

'I've also done modern plays, which I've enjoyed immensely. I just don't want to throw my career away doing crap sitcoms for ten years, make a whole lot of money, buy a big house in the country and then look back at what I had done with regret. Although, if a great film came along with a fantastic script, I wouldn't rule it out. It's just that I became an actor to act. I don't want to be a puppet or some guy who's there to fulfil a function. I want to be there with all the complexity that goes on in people's lives.'

Adrian lives in London with his American actress-turned-psychotherapist wife, Michele, and their eight-year-old daughter, Anna. But before he settled down, Adrian was something of a globetrotter, and spent three years travelling through Australia, South Malaysia and India after gaining a drama degree at Hull University. Later, he even went to Los Angeles with his wife and child in the hope of finding work. 'I enjoyed being out there,' says Adrian, 'but it's very hard. It is often the graveyard for the aspirations of Brits who go over there trying to bust in.'

1997

Will Preston, Erica Matthews and Andrew Attwood, who led *Peak Practice* through another successful run in 1996, returned for a fifth series. The departure of Simon Shepherd after four episodes to star in his own series, *Bliss*, saw Adrian Lukis – fresh from his portrayal of Wickham in the popular serial *Pride and Prejudice* – brought in as Dr David Shearer. His wife, Clare, who suffered a nervous breakdown three years earlier, was played by Yolanda Vazquez – previously seen on television in programmes such as *Capital City*, Agatha Christie's *Poirot*, *The Bill* and *A Touch of Frost* – after first choice Fiona Gillies was unable to accept the part because she was about to have a baby. However, Fiona was to take over the role the following year.

'Simon Shepherd didn't actually want to appear in any of the fifth series,' reveals Michele Buck, who continued as producer. 'But, since I had come back the previous year and he found he trusted my judgement on his character and storylines, Simon and I had developed quite a close relationship.

'He was about to make *Bliss* and didn't really need *Peak Practice*, but I told him that I wanted Will to introduce a new character because, if Dr Will says Dr David is OK, the audience will say he is OK. I told Simon I needed him for four episodes and he eventually said he would do two, which was four weeks' work. So I then said: "What if I do your workload for four episodes in four weeks?" He said: "I'll do it!" So we shot Simon's scenes for four episodes out of sequence.'

The vehicle for Simon's departure was the birth of a daughter to Will and his girlfriend, Dr Kate Webster. The couple married and left Cardale after baby Emily was diagnosed with cystic fibrosis and she was offered treatment by a research unit in Bristol that could improve the quality of her life.

When the new series of 14 episodes started, Andrew was seen returning to The Beeches six months after leaving Will and Erica in the lurch by taking locum work at an inner-city practice in Moss Side, Manchester, following his marriage break-up and nervous breakdown. David Shearer was soon having troubles of his own, dealing with the increasingly irrational behaviour of his wife, Clare, and her admission to a psychiatric hospital. Meanwhile, Erica admitted her attraction to Andrew, but refused to commit herself until she had found her natural parents.

Issues such as epilepsy, leukaemia, artificial insemination, Parkinson's disease and ovarian cancer were covered during the series. Another arrival in the cast was Joy Brook in the role of The Beeches' new receptionist, Joanne Pearson, after TV roles in *The Thin Blue Line*, *Band of Gold* and *Dalziel and Pascoe*.

Adrian Lukis joined Saskia Wickham, Simon Shepherd and Gary Mavers in the fifth series.

THE CHARACTERS

DR WILL PRESTON (Simon Shepherd)
The Beeches' senior partner, Will is stronger personally and professionally than ever before and has found happiness with Dr Kate Webster. But their joy at the birth of baby Emily soon switches to heartache.

DR ERICA MATTHEWS
(Saskia Wickham)
Putting her love life on hold, Erica throws her energies into working at The Beeches and doing up a rundown cottage. She often finds herself holding the balance of power during the frequent clashes between Andrew and newly arrived David.

DR ANDREW ATTWOOD
(Gary Mavers)
After walking out on Will and Erica as he was about to sign a partnership agreement, Andrew returns to The Beeches after six months away in Manchester. His hope of being accepted back into the fold is threatened by the arrival of Will's old friend, Dr David Shearer.

DR DAVID SHEARER (Adrian Lukis)
Invited to join The Beeches by his old friend Will, local boy David returns to his native Derbyshire with wife Clare and children Emma and Tom. He has doubts about joining a fundholding practice but, after working as a locum, becomes a partner.

DR KATE WEBSTER
(Shelagh McLeod)
After initially being irritated by Will's attempts to force the pace of their relationship, Kate has become pregnant and decided to keep the baby. But there are testing times ahead after the birth.

CLARE SHEARER (Yolanda Vazquez)
Arriving in Cardale three years after suffering a nervous breakdown, the behaviour of David's wife, Clare, becomes increasingly irrational.

KIM BEARDSMORE (Esther Coles)
In addition to her duties as practice manager, Kim has become fund manager following Russ Skinner's departure. But she has to relinquish her extra responsibilities when Andrew decides that spending needs to be controlled more vigorously.

LAURA ELLIOTT (Veronica Roberts)
Since her arrival as practice nurse, Laura has become well-liked by both staff and patients. She finds an ally in David on the issue of night cover, when the idea of a co-op of practices means that patients could be treated by doctors they do not know.

JOANNE PEARSON (Joy Brook)
The Beeches' new receptionist, Joanne, has an eye for Dr Andrew Attwood and makes it clear that she wants to look after him following the break-up of his marriage.

JAMES and CHLOE WHITE
(Richard Platt and Hazel Ellerby)
Following their decision to foster Gary Simms, The Manor Hotel landlord and landlady, James and Chloë, find themselves also providing accommodation to Gary's elder brother, Lee.

ALICE NORTH (Margery Mason)
Waiting for a gall bladder operation, Alice is a victim of The Beeches' need to cut costs when she is put on St Bede's Hospital's waiting list.

LEFT IN THE LURCH

Andrew had quit Cardale on the morning he was supposed to sign a partnership agreement. A second blow was struck when fund manager Russ Skinner accepted an administrative post in a kibbutz in Israel, leaving Will and Erica to steer The Beeches through some of its most difficult times. They had struggled to get along with Dr Robert, The Beeches' new locum, and cut services to meet their budget. Although Will was a very good GP, money was not his forte and The Beeches faced serious financial problems.

When Andrew arrived back at The Beeches after six months working as a locum in a Manchester inner-city practice, following his marriage break-up and a nervous breakdown, he received a frosty reception. Erica told Andrew that they were managing well without him and that Will had asked David Shearer, an old friend, to join the partnership.

Defeated, Andrew returned to Manchester, but he hated the conveyor-belt approach to patient consultations and returned to Cardale, where he pleaded for a hearing with Will and Erica. But Will did not trust Andrew any more

- The birth of Will Preston and Kate Webster's daughter, Emily, provided a warming opening to the series, although the later discovery that the baby suffered from cystic fibrosis added a touch of tragedy.

'We filmed the *Peak Practice* birth in Derby Hospital and used a baby who was just 24 hours old to play Emily,' reveals Shelagh McLeod, who played Kate. 'The baby's mum came up from the ward to watch, so it was quite a crowd in the delivery room with all the film crew too!'

In later episodes, the part of baby Emily was played by three eight-week-old triplets. 'They were so good,' recalls Shelagh. 'For me, triplets would be my worst nightmare and just never-ending work and sleepless nights, but their parents were so even-tempered and cool about it.'

Will and Kate's happiness at the birth of daughter Emily is short-lived, as they discover she is suffering from cystic fibrosis.

and ignored his assertion that he would be the best person to sort out The Beeches' financial problems. David then arrived for a meeting about joining the partnership.

Fate dealt a hand in keeping Andrew in Cardale when The Beeches locum resigned, Will needed to go on paternity leave when girlfriend Dr Kate Webster gave birth to their daughter Emily, and David was unsure about investing his future in a fundholding practice. Will offered Andrew the partnership and David agreed to stand in as locum while Will was away.

BATTLE OVER JENNY

When Margaret and Peter Shaw's daughter, Liz Mellor, died from cancer, they were concerned how son-in-law Steve would cope with caring for their epileptic granddaughter, Jenny. The ten-year-old's seizures had worsened since her mother's death and Steve was finding it difficult to deal with his loss, the garage that he ran and his stepchild's condition.

Margaret, who believed that Steve had not given Liz enough care, sought custody of Jenny, whom Steve had looked after from the age of four. When social services asked Erica for her opinion of Steve's ability to care for Jenny, she had to admit that Steve did have problems, but added that he was a caring father and asked for a week to allow her to work with him before any decision was made.

When Jenny had a fit at school and teachers were unable to contact him, the school called in her grandparents, who took her home. Steve snatched Jenny back and planned to run away with her. In the panic, the girl had a serious seizure and fell, smashing her head on a concrete floor. Calling by to apologise for leaving Liz during her treatment for the cancer, Andrew – on his way back to Manchester – swiftly moved into action and drove them to hospital. Jenny regained consciousness and her condition stabilised.

The incident made the whole family realise that their rowing had probably aggravated Jenny's condition. Margaret and Peter decided to call a truce with Steve and cancel the custody order.

• **Frances White** acted Margaret Shaw, who worried about her epileptic granddaughter, Jenny, after her daughter, Liz Mellor, died of cancer. She is best known as Vera Flood in the sitcom *May to December* and also acted Andrea Warner in *Raging Calm*, Kate Hamilton in *Crossroads* and Dorothy in *A Very Peculiar Practice*.

NOT SO LUCKY JIM

Erica was plagued with calls from Jim Barraclough, who was convinced that he had a stomach ulcer. When he felt that she was paying him too little attention, he took matters into his own hands and called for an ambulance to take him to hospital. Erica later visited Jim with an apology after being told by the hospital consultant that he was suffering from kidney stones.

A PRICE WORTH PAYING

Andrew spurred headteacher Bill Jackson on to fight for the survival of Cardale Primary School when it was threatened with closure. When the head, who suffered from high blood pressure, visited Andrew at The Beeches, the doctor switched Bill's prescription back to the beta blockers that he had previously been on because they were cheaper than the drugs prescribed by Erica in his absence. But Erica won support from David when she insisted it was not in patients' interests to downgrade drugs.

Bill pressed ahead with a 'Save Our School' march and fête, despite suffering dizzy spells and nose bleeds. On the day of the fête, he collapsed and hit his head on a washbasin in the men's toilets, and Andrew later apologised to him. The beta blockers were creating severe side effects that might have been exacerbated by the extra stress of running the campaign – which turned out to be successful when the school was saved from closure.

• Jim Barraclough, who thought he had an ulcer but turned out to be suffering from kidney stones, was played by **Bryan Pringle**, whose roles over the years have been as diverse as Cheese 'n' Egg in the sixties sitcom *The Dustbinmen* to pathologist Felix Norman in *Prime Suspect* and Sadly Stan Potter in *Wokenwell*.

• **Tom Georgeson**, previously seen as Eddie in *The Manageress* and Inspector Harry Naylor in *Between the Lines*, acted primary school headmaster Bill Jackson, who suffered high blood pressure.

Headteacher Bill Jackson (Tom Georgeson) battles to save Cardale Primary School from closure and to keep his high blood pressure at bay as Andrew prescribes cheaper drugs.

POORLY PAUL'S LEUKAEMIA AGONY

David was enjoying his first days back in the area when he ran into former patient Linda Kelsey, who worked in the village stores. Tragedy struck the Kelsey family when 11-year-old son Paul, whom David had delivered, was diagnosed with leukaemia.

Paul was suffering from dizzy spells and a cough, and David reassured Linda that Paul's symptoms were probably caused by a chest virus. Having spotted Paul stealing cigarettes from the shop earlier in the day, David took the boy to task about smoking. When Paul reacted with indifference, David told his mother.

After a subsequent nose bleed, Andrew noticed bruising on Paul's body and began to suspect leukaemia. When blood tests revealed that he might have the disease, David delivered the news that Paul must go to hospital. This was made even more urgent when the boy fell from the coal-shed roof, where he had been fossil hunting in the pouring rain. In hospital, doctors discovered that he had contracted pneumonia.

When bone marrow tests confirmed that Paul was suffering from cancer, doctors prepared him for chemotherapy treatment. Against the consultant's advice, Linda insisted that Paul should not be told about his illness – and was angry when David eventually revealed all to Paul, who was upset at being kept in the dark. However, he bravely faced up to his illness.

HEARTBREAK FOR WILL AND KATE

The birth of Will and Kate's baby daughter, Emily, turned out to be a bittersweet affair.

Kate found it difficult to cope with the baby's constant crying and Will, concerned that Kate had postnatal depression, asked David to talk to her. But David was taken aback by Emily's high temperature and called a paediatrician. Hospital tests revealed that she was suffering from cystic fibrosis – a congenital illness that affects the lungs and functioning of the pancreas – and a build-up of mucous on her chest had developed into pneumonia.

Kate and Will were devastated and their fragile relationship was tested to the limit. Kate, over-emotional, told Will that they had no hope of a future together because everything they touched seemed to go wrong. But David made a brokenhearted Will understand that Kate really did need him. He told the couple to fight for Emily and recommended that they get her on a research programme in Bristol.

After meeting doctors there, Kate and Will agreed to move away from Cardale. Making an honest man of Will, Kate arranged a secret register office wedding with two strangers for witnesses. They then invited all their friends from The Beeches to a reception back at their home before leaving for Bristol.

AND DAVID MAKES THREE...

When Will and Kate announced their departure, David agreed to become a partner at The Beeches and moved his family – Spanish wife Clare and children Emma and Tom – to Cardale. It was like coming home for David, who had been born in the neighbouring village of Braisewell. He regarded it as a wonderful opportunity to raise a family in beautiful surroundings.

The couple found their dream home in a

David Shearer (Adrian Lukis) brings wife Clare (Yolanda Vazquez) and children Emma and Tom (Jenni Gallagher and Nicholas Harvey) to Cardale as he becomes a partner at The Beeches.

remote stone farmhouse with outbuildings and land, where Clare planned to plant an orchard and grow vegetables. One day David returned home to find a cow that Clare had bought from the Gillespies, local dairy farmers, grazing outside the house. Clare explained that it was bound to save them lots of money because they drank so much milk.

At The Beeches, Andrew, Erica and David worked well together, but Andrew often found himself out in the cold after taking on the role of fund manager. Erica and David's main concern was that cost cutting should not be detrimental to their patients.

Sparks flew when Andrew insisted – to Erica's consternation – that cheaper drugs should be prescribed to save money. But Andrew doggedly began to turn The Beeches round by wheeler-dealing for the best hospital contracts and taking on company medical contracts.

SILVER LINING HAS A CLOUD

When elderly Derek Lomas won a trip up the Amazon, he was not sure whether to be delighted or terrified – he had a phobia about needles and he knew that he would need a course of holiday jabs. After fleeing from The Beeches terrified at his first attempt, Derek decided to try again. Fate intervened when he fainted, giving Andrew and nurse Laura the chance to carry out the deed.

• Derek Lomas, who needed holiday jabs for his prize-winning trip up the Amazon, was played by **Ewan Hooper**, best known as Det. Sgt Smith in the seventies police series *Hunter's Walk*.

ALICE FEARS SURGERY

Alice North's wait for a gall bladder operation was made even longer when she failed to open the letter confirming her admission to St Bede's, so terrified was she at the prospect. When Erica discovered this, she persuaded Alice to undergo the surgery.

But, shortly after being admitted to hospital, the pensioner was sent packing when emergency admissions took priority. An irate Erica tackled Andrew, who had entered The Beeches into a contract with St Bede's instead of the County Hospital, with which they had previously dealt, because it offered a more 'competitive' price.

When Alice collapsed while feeding her chickens, Erica sent her to the County. Her gallstone had perforated the bile duct, and led to peritonitis, an inflammation of the lining of the internal abdominal wall. Erica then cancelled The Beeches' contract with St Bede's. As a result, St Bede's offered The Beeches a better deal, claiming it had made an administrative error.

- Two days after undergoing a gall bladder operation in her role as Alice North in *Peak Practice* – in fact, the second such operation faced by Alice in the programme! – actress Margery Mason was facing the same treatment as Myrtle Fairley in the first episode of the ITV romantic drama series *Reckless*, starring Robson Green and Francesca Annis.

When she was rushed to the County Hospital for surgery, **Rupert Wickham** – actor brother of *Peak Practice* star Saskia – shared the screen with his sister for the first time when he took the role of Dr Peter Cope, an accident and emergency houseman who examined Alice.

Andrew Secombe, actor son of entertainer and presenter Sir Harry, was once a presenter of *Play School* and, since his *Peak Practice* appearance as Dr Alan Stark at the County Hospital, has been seen as a vicar in *The Detectives*.

In the same episode, an old man was played by **Hugh Munro**, who was a top director in the early days of ITV and has since become a character actor in programmes such as *The Bill*, *Pie in the Sky* and *Wycliffe*.

RUDGE FUDGES ALLERGIES

David was dealt a double dose of the Rudge family when Dawn and her brood visited The Beeches twice to complain about their intolerance to cow's milk and wheat. Dawn insisted that they should be given an expensive dietary prescription, but David said this was both costly and unnecessary.

To pacify her, David took a video of a patient with gluten enteropathy – a serious intolerance to wheat – undergoing surgery to Dawn's home for her family to watch. This rapidly changed their minds about having the condition and they decided that they were all in excellent health.

ANDREW IN CRASH HORROR

When Beeches staff planned a surprise 30th-birthday party for Erica at the Shearers' home, Clare prepared the food as Andrew set off to collect duty-free wine from a friend. As he made his way back across the snowy moors, his car broke down. Andrew found a nearby telephone box to let David know.

Then angina sufferer Frank Gladstone arrived and offered to tow Andrew to the nearest garage. As he began to manoeuvre his car into position, a lorry careered round the bend and smashed into Frank's car, which in turn knocked Andrew's vehicle into the telephone box. Frank was left trapped in his car and both Andrew and Joey, the lorry driver, were injured.

After escaping from his cab, a dazed Joey ran back to his vehicle to get help. But the cab exploded into flames as he switched on the ignition, transforming him into a human torch. Andrew dashed to put out the flames and used Erica's birthday wine to sterilise Joey's wounds as he sat shivering with shock at the roadside.

Special effects created a huge explosion following a car crash in a scene filmed over five days in sub-zero temperatures around Castleton, Derbyshire.

• Some of *Peak Practice*'s most dramatic scenes came with a car accident on icy roads after Andrew Attwood dashed off to collect some duty-free wine from a friend for a surprise 30th-birthday party organised for Erica by The Beeches staff. The crash left Andrew with head injuries, an angina sufferer trapped in his car and a lorry driver dead.

The filming took place in Castleton, Derbyshire, over five particularly bad winter nights in November 1996. 'The conditions were hideous,' says *Peak Practice* producer Michele Buck. 'We had freezing fog and so much snow the crew were snowed in for two days! Then the blizzards stopped and we hired snow machines to ensure continuity in each scene.

'On film, the blazing vehicles against the snowy backdrop look spectacular, but I can assure you, making this episode was a gruesome experience!'

Contending with sub-zero temperatures, some of the actors wore thermal underwear and had to ensure that they did not end up in trouble themselves. 'In one scene, Jack Deam, who played the lorry driver, was almost naked,' says Michele. 'We had a nurse standing by and she warned us that five minutes' exposure to the intense cold is the limit before hypothermia sets in.'

Four cameras stood by to film the stunt, which was co-ordinated by **Alan Stuart**. 'You have to have the right people for a stunt that requires such precision,' says Alan. 'I insisted on using Dave Bickers, who is one of the finest riggers of stunt vehicles in the world. We also had a stunt double for each vehicle's driver.

'When we shot the car squashing into Andrew's vehicle, which then crashed into the telephone box, we filmed it first without the second car hitting the box. Dave had to bolt Andrew's car down so that it didn't move while filming that sequence, then we put it on wires to get it into the telephone box.

'The stunt driver in the truck had to hit the first car spot-on so that it went on to hit the other car. Then, Gary Mavers's double had to time it so that he fell over at the right time.

'I used Dave Beavis for the special effects, which came in when the lorry driver tried to restart his vehicle and the cabin went up in flames. Everything was wired up to a battery and, on a signal, Dave ignited it electrically by pressing the button at the right moment.'

Frank Gladstone, the angina sufferer trapped in his car in the middle of the carnage, was played by **Allan Surtees**, who has appeared in films such as *10 Rillington Place*, *Get Carter* and *Erik the Viking* and on television in *The Professionals*, *The Bill*, *Pie in the Sky* and as Ron Dixon's bigamous father Cyril in *Brookside*.

The consultant who gave Erica and David the news that Andrew's brain scan was clear after the accident was played by **Glyn Grain** during the middle of his run in *Coronation Street* as Liz McDonald's ex-jailbird lover, Fraser Henderson.

Stunt co-ordinator Alan Stuart and special effects man Dave Beavis were also on hand when Erica's cottage went up in smoke at the end of the series.

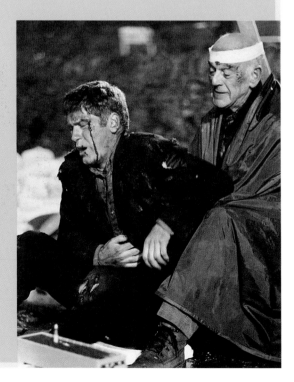

As David set off from Cardale to locate Andrew, Frank suffered a heart attack and Andrew tried to resuscitate him. The doctor also had to give a sedative to Joey, who was becoming hysterical at the thought that he would be responsible for Frank's death.

When David arrived, his defibrillator – a piece of electronic equipment designed to give electro-shocks to the heart – was not charged, so he called Erica, who had just arrived outside the Shearers' home, where the party revellers were hiding inside. Erica turned round and headed straight off for the scene of the accident with her apparatus and, with David, managed to revive Frank. Joey was already dead from a ruptured spleen. Erica also calmed down Andrew, who was hysterical and gasping for air.

On the way to hospital in an ambulance, Andrew – despite suffering from a collapsed lung himself – performed a pericardial aspiration to drain the blood that had built up around Frank's heart. Once Andrew's condition stabilised in hospital, Erica visited him and he presented her with a belated birthday present – a novelty calculator.

BELOW & LEFT
Andrew is injured in a car accident with elderly angina sufferer Frank Gladstone (Allan Surtees), who later suffers a heart attack and is revived by Erica as David looks on.

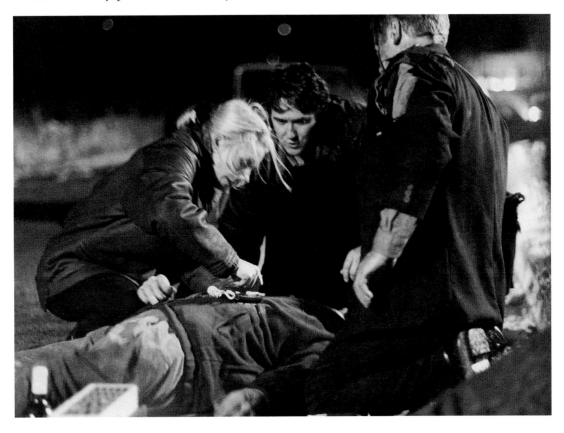

THE BEECHES AID PREGNANCY

Dairy farmer Nick Gillespie's wife, Sally, bore the brunt of the work when her husband was paralysed in a motorbike accident. Desperate to have a baby, Sally went on an Artificial Insemination by Donor (AID) programme organised by The Beeches, but Nick felt emasculated by the thought of Sally becoming pregnant by another man's sperm.

Erica was called out to the farm to treat yet another of his urinary tract infections. She felt that they were caused by poor hygiene brought on by depression. When Nick was rushed to hospital after the infection spread to his kidneys, David said Erica should have prescribed antibiotics earlier.

Andrew and Erica informed David that The Beeches would be unable to fund a fourth AID attempt if the couple's third one

- **Eva Pope**, who as Sally Gillespie ran a dairy farm with wheelchair-bound husband Nick and was devastated by their failed attempts to have a child, is best remembered for her role as *Coronation Street* barmaid Tanya Pooley, who had affairs with Des Barnes and his boss, Alex Christie, at the same time before running off with Bet Gilroy's lorry driver boyfriend Charlie Whelan. She has also appeared in *Men of the World*, *Ellington* and *Heartbeat*, and acted in the acclaimed film *Under the Skin*.

Nick, struggling to come to terms with his disability following an accident, was played by **Con O'Neill**, previously seen as Jed in *The Riff Raff Element* and Nick in the sitcom *Moving Story*, as well as Peter in the film *Dancin' Thru the Dark*. He subsequently acted Capt. Blifil in *The History of Tom Jones: A Foundling*.

Royal Shakespeare Company actress **Suzanne Bertish**, who has been seen in many character parts on TV and acted Mirav Levison in the third series of *Love Hurts*, was seen as Dr Brodie.

In the same episode, **Patsy Byrne** took the role of hypochondriac Mrs Burns after acting Nursie in *Blackadder II* and and *Blackadder's Christmas Carol*, and Mrs Stoneway in seven series of the sitcom *Watching*.

failed. Fortunately, Sally's pregnancy test proved positive. She was elated, but a severely depressed Nick disappeared into the fields and washed down a bottle of pills with vodka.

Paralysed Nick Gillespie (Con O'Neill) feels emasculated when wife Sally (Eva Pope) goes on an Artificial Insemination by Donor programme.

Found by Sally just in time, he was rushed to hospital, where he refused to speak to his wife. On his discharge, Nick stayed with the Shearers. It was only when Sally began to bleed and was admitted to hospital that Nick realised what he faced losing. Fortunately, the foetus was found to be in good health and Sally and Nick were reconciled.

BABY'S SYMPTOMS PUZZLE ERICA

Christine Higson and her salesman husband Joe had recently moved to Cardale after the cot death of their first child, Jessica. Christine felt lonely and abandoned by Joe, whose job often took her away from home. Their two-year-old son, Daniel, had been in and out of hospital for much of his brief life. In Cardale, Erica was left puzzled

Münchausen by Proxy sufferer Christine Higson (Ruth Gemmell) fakes son Daniel's illnesses when left on her own by travelling salesman husband Joe (Ray Stevenson).

• The drama of baby Daniel Higson, whose apparent illness baffled The Beeches' doctors, combined with the practice's attempts to persuade another surgery to form a co-op, brought to the screen in one episode two married couples as guest stars.

Ruth Gemmell and **Ray Stevenson**, who met while playing tragic couple Gina and Steve Dixon in *Band of Gold* and eventually married in November 1997, acted Daniel's parents, Christine and Joe. Ruth has also played Det. Constable Kerry Cox in the first series of *Silent Witness*, alongside former *Peak Practice* star Amanda Burton, and Colin Firth's girlfriend in the film *Fever Pitch*. Ray, the only actor to appear in two Catherine Cookson TV adaptions – *The Dwelling Place* and *The Tide of Life* – has since starred as Det. Insp. Tony Baynham in the BBC police series *City Central*.

Husband and wife **Jennifer Wilson** and **Brian Peck**, who married in 1959, played Dr Baxter and Dr Geoffrey Smith, whose Bridgport practice was approached by The Beeches' doctors with a view to forming a co-op with them and others to give night cover to patients. Jennifer is still remembered for her role as

when Christine brought him in with diarrhoea and vomiting. She diagnosed gastroenteritis, but the symptoms disappeared within hours.

Andrew's hunch that Christine was suffering from Münchausen by Proxy – creating the symptoms – was eventually proved correct when Erica found salt in one of Daniel's feeding bottles. Christine admitted her illness to Joe and, reported by the doctors, was taken away by the police and a social worker.

BUSMAN CRASHES OUT OF RACE

Miner-turned-bus driver Stan Jordan was a keen marathon runner who trained for a charity 10km run with David, who struggled to keep up with him. So David was surprised when Stan's fitness was questioned by his disliked boss, Lou Collinson – who cancelled a much-needed bus service in the village – as part of the depot's contract with The Beeches.

Collinson felt that Stan, who had experienced a few minor scrapes with the buses, was past it, and wanted to get rid of him. He was disappointed when David gave his employee a clean bill of health. Angered by Collinson's attitude, David cancelled The Beeches' lucrative contract, and an annoyed Andrew threatened to set up consultancy work of his own with the depot.

Ignoring the birth of his first grandchild – have fallen out with his daughter, Ruth, ten years earlier over her husband Martin's role in the union split during the miners' strike – Stan concentrated on preparations for the run. But while training with David, he fell and hurt his arm. On being told by Stan's wife, Joyce, that he had been very tired and stiff recently, the GP worried that Stan had Parkinson's disease.

Andrew came to the same conclusion after a school bus driven by Stan ran off the road. Collinson fired him and threatened to sue David for professional negligence over the medical. But one of the bus owner's mechanics told Andrew that Stan's bus had been unfit to drive. David helped Stan to face up to his illness and he returned home to Joyce, where he told her that he wanted to see Ruth again.

Jenny Hammond in *The Brothers* in the seventies. Brian has appeared in dozens of television series, including *Dixon of Dock Green*, *Z Cars*, *Rising Damp*, *Minder*, *The Bill*, *Last of the Summer Wine* and *London's Burning*.

● Veteran screen actor **Kenneth Colley**, who played miner-turned-bus driver Stan Jordan, has appeared in films such as *The Jokers*, *How I Won the War*, *Monty Python's Life of Brian*, *The Empire Strikes Back*, *Return of the Jedi* and *A Summer Story*. His many television roles include Jack Moss in the sixties series *The Plane Makers* and Ken Uttley in the nineties sitcom *Moving Story*.

ANDREW'S TANGLED LOVE LIFE

Since returning to The Beeches, Andrew had been keen to put down roots in Cardale, and had found a place to rent. He was not able to buy because he had ploughed his money into the partnership and was paying the college fees for his estranged wife, Kirsty.

Footloose and fancy-free, he was soon dating Joanne Pearson, The Beeches' new receptionist, who told Andrew

that she wanted a relationship with 'strings' attached. The final straw came when Joanne wanted to take Andrew home to meet her parents. He backed off quickly and told her that he needed breathing space. Joanne was upset and their relationship fizzled out.

Andrew began spending more time with Erica, helping out with the DIY at the cottage she had bought for renovation. Although the pair often rowed, a definite attraction existed between them. He invited her to a disastrous dinner at which the nervous Liverpudlian ended up offending Erica with his muddled declaration of love. Erica misunderstood and marched off in a huff. Andrew then fell for health authority accountant Gina Johnson, and the pair began a passionate but short-lived affair based purely on sex.

Andrew falls for the charms of The Beeches' receptionist Joanne Pearson (Joy Brook).

AGONY FOR ANDREW'S PAL

- Seven-year-old **Abby Mavers** joined father Gary in one episode of *Peak Practice* as Toni Young, daughter of Andrew's best friend, Phil, who turned up from Liverpool when he was dying from a berry aneurysm. In real life, Gary and **Mark Moraghan**, who played Phil, are good friends and Mark has since become a regular in *Brookside* as builder Greg Shadwick.

It was Abby's first acting role and she told her father afterwards: 'I'm going to be an actress when I grow up. You get to do all my favourite things, like dressing up and pretending to be someone else – and then you get paid for it!'

Abby, Gary's daughter from a seven-year relationship that ended before he married his make-up artist wife Sue, was spotted by *Peak Practice*'s casting director when she visited her father on location.

Paddy Joyce was seen as old people's home resident Mr Austen – suffering from asthma when Phil Young followed Andrew on his calls – after a long career of acting in programmes such as *Cathy Come Home*, *The Saint*, *Pennies from Heaven*, *Softly Softly*, *Minder*, *Lovejoy* and *The Bill*. He also acted John Royle, father of Queen Vic landlord Eddie, in *EastEnders*.

Andrew's old friend Phil Young arrived in Cardale with only days to live after being told that he had a berry aneurysm (a weakness of the wall of the arteries in his brain). Married with a young daughter called Toni, Phil had driven from his Liverpool home in the middle of the night without telling his wife that he was dying.

Andrew was shocked to hear of his friend's fate and agreed to go to Australia with Phil, who had bought them both a one-way ticket to the country that had been their dream destination when they were younger. Once at the airport, Phil backed out after seeing a girl his daughter's age. It made him realise that he could not leave his family.

Andrew followed Phil into a club where the two of them sang in a karaoke. Then he drove Phil back home to his wife, Carol, after a night spent in the car. Andrew was left to deliver the bad news, with Phil too upset to talk.

Andrew is glad to see old friend Phil Young (Mark Moraghan) from Liverpool but shattered to learn that he has just days to live.

THEY'RE ALL IN THE CO-OP!

When the Brompton Health Centre pulled out of its shared night-call arrangement, using a deputising service instead, Erica suggested that The Beeches should join a co-op of practices rather than go back to the old way of covering all night calls themselves.

She carefully costed the venture and Andrew agreed to a trial run. They found several other practices to join them, despite the opposition of David and practice nurse Laura, who did not like the idea of farming their patients out to strangers who knew nothing about them.

These fears turned out to be well-founded when Paul Kelsey – whose leukaemia was in remission – ended up gravely ill in hospital again after a co-op doctor, unfamiliar with his condition, made a wrong decision.

Paul had caught chickenpox, but when his mother, Linda, got the boy's white cell count wrong, the co-op doctor told her there was nothing to worry about. Paul was soon in hospital, with the rash covering his eyes and mouth. The Kelsey family were devastated on being told that Paul's leukaemia had returned. David was fuming and persuaded Erica to pull out of the co-op arrangement.

arranged a meeting with the owner of a local animal sanctuary, who later offered her a job.

After Susan's drug addict boyfriend, Mark, arrived in the village, Erica took blood tests from both of them. Although Mark was clear, Susan's revealed that she had hepatitis. When receptionist Joanne refused to hand over her daily methadone dose in Erica's absence and Andrew threw her out, Susan broke into The Beeches to get her fix.

Susan overdosed on the methadone she had stolen from The Beeches and ended up in hospital, where her father visited her after a plea from Erica. As they talked, Susan was able to bury some of her demons and, on her discharge, appeared to turn over a new leaf by dumping Mark. She now had everything she wanted in Cardale – a job with animals and her father.

- Young actress **Keeley Forsyth**, who played Trish – a nurse in the hospital to which hepatitis sufferer Susan Jakes was admitted after a drugs overdose – previously acted in *Children's Ward* and took the role of Nicky in two series of *The Biz*. She has since appeared in *Where the Heart Is* and *Hollyoaks*.

TOUGH LOVE

Methadone addict Susan Jakes arrived in Cardale to find the father who had abandoned her as a baby after her mother's death. Noticing an abscess on her arm caused by using dirty needles, Erica pledged to help Susan by placing her on a withdrawal programme. When she learned of Susan's wish to work with animals, Erica

CLARE'S CARDALE COLOUR...

Quickly settling into Cardale, Clare Shearer organised the village's annual pageant, held in memory of St Rosamund of Cardale. James White decided to bowl the maidens over in his old knight's costume, but he was horrified to discover he had piled on the pounds since he last wore it. He tried to shed them but, after The Beeches doctors

all gave him different advice, he failed to lose any weight. He stopped when Chloë told James that she was happy with him the way he was. The pageant was a great success, although Clare was left rather hurt by snide comments about her 'ridiculous' manner.

Receptionist Joanne Pearson, practice nurse Laura Elliott (Veronica Roberts) and practice manager Kim Beardsmore enjoy the Cardale pageant.

...AND WORRYING BEHAVIOUR

After Sylvia Gadd's long overdue operation to remove a cataract from her eye, she was warned to adjust slowly to normal life and be careful of infection. On a picnic with Clare Shearer, who unknown to her was ill with manic depression, Clare accidentally poked Sylvia in the eye as she inspected her new lens. Sylvia began to feel increasingly uneasy as Clare babbled away in Spanish.

Hurt by Sylvia's manner, the doctor's wife angrily started up the car, which lurched forward and caused Sylvia to smash her head on the dashboard. Failing to show Sylvia any compassion, Clare dropped her at her home, leaving

- Cataract patient Sylvia Gadd was acted by **Colette O'Neil**, who had played Len Fairclough's girlfriend Ruth Winter in *Coronation Street* in the mid-sixties. She has also been seen on television in *Couples*, as Sheila Warner, the Beryl Bainbridge play *Blue Skies from Now On*, *Bulman*, *Lovejoy*, *Casualty* and *Hamish*

her to phone for a doctor. At the hospital, it was discovered that the bump had dislodged her new lens and that she needed further surgery.

David had tried to ignore Clare's irrational behaviour for some time in the hope that it would go away, but when it persisted he became increasingly concerned. Then, one day, he arrived home in the nick of time to stop Clare – who had become obsessed about hygiene – throwing a full can of diesel on a bonfire of her burning crockery, clothes and furniture. David comforted his terrified children and called for Andrew, the only person she would talk to.

Andrew convinced David that Clare's manic depression made her a danger to herself and others and that she must be admitted to a psychiatric hospital. She was sick and needed urgent help. This episode helped to break down any barriers that had existed between David and Andrew.

Macbeth. The Scottish actress has the distinction of appearing in both the original sixties series *Dr Finlay's Casebook* and the nineties revival *Doctor Finlay*.

In the same episode, Clare Shearer's head of department at the university, Mike Walton, was played by **David McAlister**, who took the role of Matthew Palmer in the sitcom *Growing Pains*. He is often cast as policemen.

David comforts his children after arriving home to find manic depressive wife Clare setting fire to crockery, clothes and furniture.

HEALER NEEDS HEALING HANDS

When Alice North was discharged early from hospital after a hip operation, The Beeches booked her a care assistant from Healing Hands, an agency run by Melissa Hollingsworth. When the astute businesswoman experienced abdominal pain herself, she was shocked to discover that she might be pregnant. She had not planned to have a baby so early in her career.

An ultrasound test later revealed that Melissa had a growth, which turned out to be ovarian cancer, and she was upset when she was advised to have a radical hys-

• Melissa Hollingsworth, a young career woman struck down by ovarian cancer, was played by **Valerie Gogan**, following her role as Robert Carlyle's girlfriend in *Hamish*

Macbeth, which came to an end when she drove off in a van and disappeared over a cliff.

Alex Hanson, who acted Melissa's husband, Alex, was familiar with medical dramas after previously appearing in *Casualty* and *Doctor Finlay*. Off screen, he lives with actress Samantha Bond, who played Miss Moneypenny in the James Bond film *GoldenEye*.

• Stuntman **Paul Weston**, who has worked on James Bond films, stood in for actor Tony Vogel when bird-watcher Freddie Fairburn was seen falling over a cliff at Blackmoor Pass and on to a ledge below, suffering head injuries. **Roy Alon** co-ordinated the stunt and the rescue operation, which involved Gary Mavers as Andrew.

Three cameras were used so that the stunt could be filmed in the minimum possible time, reducing the risks to both stuntmen and actors. Alan Grint, who directed the episode, took hold of one of the cameras himself and filmed some of the most dramatic pictures of the daring rescue.

terectomy, as she had hoped to have children one day.

The cancer appeared to bring Melissa closer to her step-daughter, Sophie, with whom she had a difficult relationship. As she came to terms with the operation, Melissa realised that, although she would never have a child of her own, she was surrounded by people who loved and needed her.

LEE'S BEAR NECESSITIES

James and Chloë were startled to find that Lee, the brother of their foster child, Gary, who was now living with them, had sleepwalked into bed with them one night. On another occasion, he sprained his ankle by tripping over some beer barrels as he patrolled outside in only his boxer shorts. When nothing seemed to stop Lee, Andrew even suggested that he handcuff himself to the bed.

His problem was eventually solved by Bee Bop, his tatty old childhood teddybear. Although Lee was annoyed with Gary for telling Andrew that the bear had sorted out his sleeping problems when he was younger, with Bee Bop tucked up beside him, Lee's nocturnal wanderings came to a halt.

BIRDS OF A FEATHER

Bird-lover Freddie Fairburn, who had walked out on his wife and son seven years earlier, lived in a squalid barn where he devoted all his time to his feathered friends. One afternoon, while following a falcon along a cliff, he fell over the edge and was knocked out.

Saved by the mountain rescue team, Freddie was taken to hospital, where X-rays revealed that he was suffering from emphysema, an incurable condition of the lungs that would worsen if he did not leave his dilapidated home.

When Andrew told Freddie's estranged wife, Nancy, of his poor health, she immediately offered him a room in her home. This outraged her new partner, Ted, and her son ,Jason, who could not forgive Freddie for leaving. Ted visited Freddie and, as a fight broke out, he floored him.

Andrew was called to tend to Freddie, who then spoke to Nancy for the first time in years. When she offered to take

'Every artist has to be locked on with wire,' says Roy Alon. 'Then they can hang out in a position that looks hazardous. Alan was in an even more potentially dangerous position than the stunt people, and gave me cause for concern. He was hanging over from the cliff getting some of the most exciting shots.'

Polly Hemingway, who acted Freddie Fairburn's estranged wife, Nancy, and in real life is divorced from actor Roy Marsden, is best known on television in recent years playing Mrs Whales in *Ain't Misbehavin'* and Lesley Bygrave in *The Locksmith*, but in the seventies she caused a stir in *Emmerdale* as Joe Sugden's married lover, Kathy Gimbel.

On TV, she also acted Gracie Fields in *Pride of Our Alley*, Nurse Phillips tending the wounded in *Coronation Street* when a lorry ploughed into the Rovers Return in 1979, and a community worker in the daytime soap *Miracles Take Longer*.

• Flying fanatic Vinnie Kern was played by **Philip Whitchurch**, who had previously acted Cyril McGregor in *The Brothers McGregor*, assistant school caretaker Castanets in *Scully* and Chief Insp. Cato in *The Bill*. He has since appeared in *Plotlands* as Billy Reed. **Sharon Duce**, best known as Jan Oliver in *Big Deal* and Pat Hollingsworth in *Growing Pains*, took the role of Vinnie's wife, Carol-Anne.

him back, he refused. But after discussing it with Andrew and Jason, he changed his mind. Ted came to terms with the situation, accepting that Nancy still loved Freddie.

FLIGHT OF DECEPTION

Vinnie Kern had an aviation business and planned for the day his son Daniel would join him in it. At the same time, he tended to ignore his other son, Stuart. Vinnie was also a secretive man. Unbeknown to his wife, Carole-Anne, he had remortgaged their home to save the business, and he had also hidden from her the fact that he had suffered from heart palpitations for years.

When Vinnie collapsed with a palpitation attack, David warned him that he could have an overactive thyroid. The following evening, when Daniel confessed to his father that he was gay, Vinnie was disgusted, hurt and very angry that Carol-Anne already knew. He had another palpitation and David was called for. Tests revealed that he was suffering from Wolfe Parkinson White syndrome, a condition where an electrical pathway in the heart can make it beat too fast. Vinnie was devastated to be told that he would not be able to fly again.

Meanwhile, Stuart had gone missing – along with Tom and Emma Shearer, who were upset after overhearing their parents rowing. Carol-Anne blamed Vinnie for driving Stuart away. He rushed to the aerodrome, where he planned to take to the skies in an attempt to find the children, but David drove after Vinnie to stop him. To the relief of both families, the children were eventually found by Clare, following her return home from hospital with medication keeping her manic depression under control. She phoned the news through to David and Vinnie at the aerodrome, where the two men were discussing their failures as fathers and husbands.

OUT WITH THE OLD...

Andrew was in for a shock when estranged wife Kirsty visited him with her baby son, Christopher. She said she had fallen out with her boyfriend, Tony, and needed time to think, but she and Andrew argued about why she would not have a baby with him but did with Tony. Andrew, knowing that they no longer belonged together, eventually called for Tony to collect Kirsty.

Estranged wife Kirsty arrives on Andrew's doorstep with son Christopher after walking out on boyfriend Tony.

...AND IN WITH THE NEW

Erica had settled down well in Cardale and had invested her money in a rundown cottage on which she started doing work. But Erica was so absorbed in searching for her natural mother that her heart simply was not in it.

So, when there was a fire at the cottage, destroying most of her possessions, she seemed to take it in her stride. The blaze was first spotted by Andrew and Laura as they drove past on their way back from a rugby match in which Andrew was injured.

Andrew was hurt that Erica had not gone to watch him play, but she later told him that the After Adoption Service had found her mother's marriage certificate and she was now on the brink of finding out who she really was.

At his invitation, Erica moved in with Andrew until she could sort out alternative accommodation. The couple finally faced up to their attraction for one another, but acknowledged that their romance would have to wait a bit longer because Erica was so emotionally involved in tracing her natural mother. The pair kissed tenderly and Andrew told her that he would be there for her when she was ready.

Andrew and Erica can contain their feelings for one another no longer, but full-blooded romance has to wait until she has traced her natural mother.

PRACTICE MAKES PERFECT

Ensuring that all medical procedures are carried out authentically on screen is the job of medical advisers Tim Parkin, a Derbyshire GP, and Helen Holmes, a qualified nurse. Tim works closely with the scriptwriters and briefs Helen on particular scenes. She is then on set to ensure that everything is carried out correctly and realistically.

Tim joined *Peak Practice* before its fifth series started after answering an advertisement in the *British Medical Journal*. 'My role is to put the medical accuracy into the programme and tame writers of wild ideas!' says Tim. 'I meet the script editors and producer when they're planning how the series and characters will develop. They ask me about issues such as fundholding, where the money comes from and whether The Beeches could afford to expand.

'Then I sit down with writers and talk through medical facts in individual episodes, how a doctor would respond to any given situation with patients, how he would examine patients, how he would feel about them and how doctors get on together.

'Correcting medical detail is usually about timing in the script. A writer might have a blood test, for example, then want the result an hour later. In reality, it takes three to four days. Sometimes I will be asked to come up with a disease that will fit a given situation involving the doctors. Other times, they will say they would like to do, perhaps, multiple sclerosis, but want an interesting way of portraying it. I do a lot of research and know a thousand times more than I did before joining *Peak Practice*!'

Occasionally, mistakes do slip through – and viewers are quick to let Tim know. 'In the 1998 series, Alice North had a gall bladder operation,' says Tim. 'Then someone wrote in to tell us that Alice had already had her gall bladder removed in the first series!'

Helen Holmes, who worked on the first series, returned to *Peak Practice* full-time when filming began on the programmes shown in 1997. Having been a nurse in Birmingham and Nottingham hospitals, she had previously worked on series such as *Boon* and *Outside Edge*.

'All the equipment we use is genuine,' says Helen, who is also on standby as the unit's nurse in case of accidents. 'Otherwise, some people watching it will know that it's a fake. I have to demonstrate to the screen doctors how to use equipment.

'I also end up demonstrating things like all the right noises to make during childbirth. When Fiona Gillies, as Clare Shearer, gave birth in the sixth series, that wasn't a problem because she had done so in real life not long beforehand.

'But there was another birth in the series where a woman experienced complications in having a baby at home, and that actress had not gone through childbirth herself.

'Also, it is my job to find babies and young children who don't have lines in the programme. We found a 10-day-old baby for that difficult birth and had to show the umbilical cord, which was clamped round its neck. To do that, we made a cord from sausages. It was a hot day in a stuffy room and keeping sausages attached to a baby's tummy was very difficult without doing any damage.'

Amanda Burton, who as Dr Beth Glover is seen here testing the blood pressure of fireman George Milton (Freddie Fletcher), and other Peak Practice *stars have been drilled in correct medical procedures.*

FIONA GILLIES
as Clare Shearer

ESTHER COLES
as Kim
Beardsmore

Taking over the role of Dr David Shearer's manic depressive wife Clare from Spanish actress Yolanda Vazquez presented Fiona Gillies with a challenge. 'Everything about her is very intense,' says Fiona. 'She's an extrovert and a very quick thinker. It's not so much difficult to play her as interesting and thought-provoking. I love the role. It's a great, tasty number. I like Clare very much. She's a wonderful, fascinating, complex person.

'To find out about manic depression, I spoke to a friend who's a clinical psychologist and she was very helpful. But all of us also had to work hard to make sure the audience completely believed that we're a family who have a history, live together, get on well and enjoy each other's company.'

Fiona had, in fact been first choice to play Clare when the role was originally cast, but she was pregnant with son Louis.

Born of Scottish parents, Fiona met actor husband Michael Mueller while working with the Royal Shakespeare Company. She previously played Angela in the BBC series *Mother Love*, Jennifer in the mini-series *A Woman's Guide to Adultery*, starring Sean Bean, a murderess in *Cadfael* and Becky Johnson in two series of the sitcom *Joking Apart*, as well as acting in the 1993 TV movie *Frankenstein*.

Landing a role in a television series set in her native Midlands meant more to Esther Coles than becoming a regular in Britain's best-loved serial, *Coronation Street*. As receptionist-turned-practice manager Kim Beardsmore, Esther is one of only four surviving members from *Peak Practice*'s original cast – and has appeared in more episodes than anyone else.

'When I joined,' explains the actress, 'I had just been in *Coronation Street* as Racquel's friend who helped her with a sexy underwear party. Then, after I filmed the first series of *Peak Practice*, they asked me to go back, but I really enjoyed this and wanted to stay.'

Esther, from Nottingham, trained at RADA after being a 'show-off' at school, then made her professional debut with the acclaimed Hull Truck Theatre Company, working with writer-director John Godber. She had small parts on television and played a nurse in the film *Second Best*. *Peak Practice* was the actress's big break, but one aspect of Kim she does not like is her clothes.

'I hate them!' says Esther. 'I think I'm the only actress in the programme who hasn't bought any of my costumes. Kim's really dumpy! In the early days, she always wore teddy-bear jumpers. It's nice to get away from yourself, but it's always a relief for me to get back into my own clothes.'

MARGERY
MASON
as Alice North

CLIVE SWIFT as
Norman Shorthose

When veteran character actress Margery Mason was offered the role of cantankerous Cardale pensioner Alice North in the first series of *Peak Practice*, she had no idea that it would become her longest-running role.

'It's been nice for me,' says Margery, 'although I almost didn't do it because, in the first episode, Alice had only one line, so I told my agent: "I'm not doing that." She said there was more in the next one, so I carried on, but I certainly didn't expect it to last for so long. I'm trying to hang on to my original characterisation of her as a really feisty old girl with a fairly soft heart who adds comic elements to the story.'

While Alice has been beset on screen with a multitude of illnesses, Margery has kept in remarkably good health. Most years, she swims 150 lengths – about eight miles – in the BT Swimathon. 'Last time, it took me three-and-a-half hours,' says the actress, who took to the stage in her mother's company at 14, touring clubs in London's East End, before moving into repertory theatre.

She went on to act in films such as *The Raging Moon*, *Charlie Bubbles*, *Pink Floyd: The Wall* and the 1998 version of *Les Miserables*. Before joining *Peak Practice*, Margery was best remembered on television for her roles in the epic series *A Family at War* and Judi Dench's mother in *Talking to a Stranger*. She has also appeared in *A Touch of Frost* and *Reckless* in recent years.

Trying to lay the ghost of Hyacinth Bucket's long-suffering husband Richard in the popular sitcom *Keeping Up Appearances*, Clive Swift turned up in *Peak Practice* as hypochondriac chemist Norman Shorthose to become a thorn in the side of The Beeches doctors.

'I took the role partly because I was so delighted to have a contrasting character to Richard,' says the Liverpool-born actor. 'That was a wonderful role, but it could have meant the end of my television career because everyone identified me so closely with the part. So I grabbed Norman Shorthose with both hands! Bearing in mind how docile Richard was, I enjoyed playing an aggressive and rude character.

Clive, who gained experience in drama societies while studying at Cambridge University at the same time as Derek Jacobi and Ian McKellen, fondly remembers his years with the Royal Shakespeare Company under Peter Hall in the sixties and working with film directors Alfred Hitchcock in *Frenzy* and David Lean in *A Passage to India*.

On television, he played Inspector Waugh in *Waugh on Crime*, and starred in *South Riding*, *Clayhanger*, *Barchester Chronicles* and *First Among Equals*. Divorced from the novelist Margaret Drabble, Clive has two sons and a daughter. He is the brother of *Drop the Dead Donkey* actor David Swift.

1998

The big question as *Peak Practice* returned to a transmission day of Monday for its sixth series, was whether Andrew Attwood and Erica Matthews would make it all the way to the altar. David Shearer, meanwhile, had to contend with his manic depressive wife becoming pregnant and coming off the medication on which she relied. Erica and Andrew's own families also featured in the story, as adopted Erica searched for her natural father and Andrew returned home to his dying mother in Liverpool.

Fiona Gillies, who had played Jennifer in the mini-series *A Woman's Guide to Adultery* and Becky Johnson in the sitcom *Joking Apart*, took over the part of David's wife, Clare, from Yolanda Vazquez. Fiona had been the original choice for the role but was due to have a baby in the middle of filming, so was unable to accept it. When contractual negotiations broke down between Carlton and Yolanda's agent for the 1998 series, Fiona stepped in. In fact, the original plan had been to kill off Clare by the end of the previous series, but producer Michele Buck fell in love with the character and kept her on.

Clive Swift, best known as Hyacinth Bucket's long-suffering husband, Richard, in the sitcom *Keeping Up Appearances*, joined the cast as hypochondriac pharmacist Norman Shorthose, whose new chemist shop in Cardale was to force the closure of the doctors' own dispensary and hit their incomes.

Thomas Lockyer, who subsequently acted in the mini-series *Merlin*, played crooked locum Nick Goodson, but the discovery of his fraud and deception cut short his run to four episodes. Sarah Parish, who had previously done an impersonation of Elizabeth Hurley in the TV show *The Saturday Night Armistice* and appeared in the award-winning West End comedy *Popcorn*, acted The Manor

Hotel's new barmaid, Dawn Rudge, a character that had been seen in one episode of the previous series. Yet another newcomer was Ludmilla Vuli as The Beeches receptionist Polly Stevens after playing a nurse in writer Kay Mellor's television film *Some Kind of Life* and a store detective in *EastEnders*.

The 14-part series tackled issues such as meningitis, Down's syndrome, parents dealing with allegations of child abuse, and euthanasia. During the filming, Michele Buck left to become controller of drama at United News & Media, which makes series such as *Where the Heart Is* and *Touching Evil*. Damien Timmer, a former writer and story editor on the programme, took over as producer.

One of the logistical tasks facing *Peak Practice* as filming began on the sixth series was scheduling scenes to allow Gary Mavers to join the rest of the team six weeks into filming, after he had finished shooting the three-part drama *The Unknown Soldier*, which was produced by Michele Buck, with Damien as script executive.

Shortly after the cast and crew finished filming *Peak Practice*, plans were under way for another series in 1999, with original producer Tony Virgo back at the helm and working on major changes to ensure the programme's continued popularity. It looked as if *Peak Practice* would see its way into the new millennium, remaining a mainstay of ITV's weekday schedule.

Saskia Wickham, Gary Mavers and Adrian Lukis became the second complete generation of doctors at The Beeches surgery in Peak Practice.

THE CHARACTERS

DR ANDREW ATTWOOD
(Gary Mavers)
When Erica finally commits herself to him, Andrew is ecstatic and settles into a new house. But then his mother is taken seriously ill, and he finds himself returning to his estranged family in Liverpool, who resent his middle-class life style.

DR ERICA MATTHEWS
(Saskia Wickham)
After tracking down her natural father, Jackie Brown, and discovering that her mother died in a car crash, Erica puts aside her previous insecurity to start a relationship with Andrew.

DR DAVID SHEARER
(Adrian Lukis)
Following wife Clare's manic depression, David fights to keep his family together as they face yet another hurdle in their marriage.

CLARE SHEARER (Fiona Gillies)
With her manic depression stabilised by medication, Clare struggles to find employment and faces a dilemma on discovering that she is pregnant.

NORMAN SHORTHOSE (Clive Swift)
Pompous hypochondriac Norman Shorthose has retired to Cardale after running chemist's shops in Derby for 30 years. He now plans to start a pharmacy in the village to keep himself busy – closing down The Beeches' dispensary in the process.

DR NICK GOODSON (Thomas Lockyer)
When Andrew leaves for Liverpool to tend his sick mother, Dr Nick Goodson arrives at The Beeches as a locum. He passes himself off as a charming widower with a tragic past, but Erica suspects there is more to him than meets the eye.

KIM BEARDSMORE (Esther Coles)
Office manager Kim, ever on the lookout for love, is taken in by new locum Nick Goodson.

LAURA ELLIOTT (Veronica Roberts)
Practice nurse Laura hopes to fulfil an ambition when she applies for a job with Voluntary Service Overseas.

JOANNE PEARSON (Joy Brook)
Receptionist Joanne's jealousy is set to seal her fate as former love Andrew falls for Erica.

POLLY STEVENS (Ludmilla Vuli)
New receptionist Polly Stevens joins The Beeches.

JAMES and CHLOE WHITE
(Richard Platt and Hazel Ellerby)
A meningitis outbreak triggers The Manor Hotel landlord and landlady James and Chloë's worst nightmare as daughter Sarah-Jane is admitted to hospital.

ALICE NORTH (Margery Mason)
Pensioner Alice is reunited with childhood friend Alby James 40 years after a bitter row between him and her late husband.

DAWN RUDGE (Sarah Parish)
Single mother Dawn Rudge faces up to life in the shadow of a killer disease but fights back to become The Manor Hotel's new barmaid.

CHANGE AT THE TOP

Damien Timmer stepped in as producer during the sixth series of *Peak Practice* when Michele Buck left to join United News & Media. He had already worked on the programme for three years as writer, story editor and story consultant.

'When the programme is successful, you have to work hard to keep it,' says Damien. 'It's easy for a long-running series to become tired. You have to work twice as hard to make each series better than the previous one.

'The producer's job is to motivate everyone for eight months of the year. The crew work incredibly long hours, getting up at 5.30am and often filming until 8pm, sometimes six days a week. They don't see their families a lot and it's quite tough.'

During the 1998 series, two new regular characters were introduced – chemist Norman Shorthose and Dawn Rudge, a single mother who had appeared in an episode of the previous series.

Medical adviser Tim Parkin reveals that Norman was introduced in order to create a story that would hit The Beeches financially. 'Damien asked me what would hit them hard and make them sweat,' says Tim. 'The biggest way of losing income was to lose their dispensary, which would account for 25 to 30 per cent of The Beeches' revenue.'

Damien has his own theory about the popularity of *Peak Practice*. 'There are very few dramas that tell intelligent but quite simple stories about very human things and with dignity, and also stories that can be very sad,' he says. 'I think viewers like the sadness of it, but it has a lot of heart as well – they like to see characters falling in love.'

A FAMILY AFFAIR

Saskia Wickham's third and final series of *Peak Practice* turned out to be a family affair, with her real life parents – actor **Jeffrey Wickham** and actress **Clair Stewart** – playing her adoptive parents. Saskia's brother, **Rupert Wickham**, reappeared as hospital doctor Peter Cope in the last episode of the series.

As Erica Matthews sought to meet her past head-on, **John Woodvine** was cast as her natural father, retired Northeast trucker Jackie Brown. The actor is remembered for his roles as Det. Insp. Witty in *Z Cars*, Det. Chief Supt John Kingdom in *New Scotland Yard* and Bobo Simpson Sr in *Finney*.

Sharp-eyed viewers would also have noticed a change in Saskia Wickham's hairstyle. 'I have always had really fine and wispy hair,' she said during filming. 'So this year I decided to use a hairpiece. I was taken along to this really swanky wigmaker in Covent Garden, London, and they made one specially for me after taking a mould of my head using clingfilm.

'It takes about 45 minutes to attach it in the mornings, but it's worth the time and the pain from the pins being jabbed into my head! I absolutely love having this long hair – it makes me feel like a mermaid.'

ERICA AND ANDREW SIZZLE

When Erica downed some Dutch courage at James and Chloë White's village barbecue, it was not only the sausages that were sizzling. Putting behind her the sadness of discovering that her real mother was dead, Erica invited Andrew to her single bed for a night of passion. When they woke in the morning, they were deliriously happy that their relationship was back on course.

The flames of romance between Erica and Andrew finally achieve more than a flicker.

David and Clare (Fiona Gillies) are relieved to welcome Emma and Tom back from a summer camp when Cardale is gripped by a meningitis scare.

MENINGITIS STRIKES CARDALE

Cardale was gripped by a meningitis scare when the killer disease struck twice in one month. Andrew, concerned that the cases were linked and an epidemic was about to descend, called on the health authority to begin a mass immunisation programme and was furious when it refused to act until there had been a number of connected cases.

Meanwhile, twins Gary and Philip Beamer joined other Cardale children on their annual summer camp. When Gary developed a raging fever, David Shearer discovered that he had meningitis; tragically, the boy died before reaching hospital. Then Philip developed the disease and The Beeches set up a 24-hour helpline to deal with villagers' fears.

The health authority only acted on parents' demands that their children should be offered vaccinations when James and Chloë White's daughter, Sarah-Jane, and David's daughter, Emma, were admitted to hospital with suspected meningitis. However, it turned out that Sarah-Jane had a viral infection, while Emma had simply been feigning illness.

DAWN BREAKS OFF AFFAIR

Mother-of-three Dawn Rudge, who was conducting an affair with a married man, Henry Lewis, was devastated when she discovered that she had breast cancer. Dawn could remember her own mother dying of the same disease and she did not want to leave her children to grow up without her. Taking no chances, she told Erica that she wanted a double mastectomy, but was later persuaded to have only the lump and surrounding tissue removed. Unfortunately, further tests revealed the cancer had spread to Dawn's lymph nodes and she needed chemotherapy and radiotherapy treatment.

• **Brian Capron** played Henry Lewis, the married man with whom Dawn Rudge was having an affair, after dozens of television roles that have included Jack in *Beryl's Lot*, Murray McCoy in *Full House*, Louis Calvino in *Class Act* and Rex Hall in *Crocodile Shoes*.

Dawn's workmate Val was played by **Mary Healey**, a character actress previously seen in the roles of Mrs Cochrane in *The Duchess of Duke Street* and Mary Peel in *The Mallens*. She caused a stir both in *Coronation Street* as Thelma James, who sent Emily Bishop's husband, Ernest, a Valentine's Day card in 1977, and in *Brookside* as Ruth Sweeney, Sinbad's natural mother, who had abandoned him at birth.

Louis Marsden, the agricultural rep who took a fancy to Dawn Rudge, was played by **Mark Powley**, who had spent five years in *The Bill* as PC Ken Melvin before playing Tom in two series of the sitcom *Next of Kin*.

Single mother Dawn Rudge (Sarah Parish), with son Shane (Niall Larua-Brooks), is shocked to hear that she has breast cancer.

Terrified by her cancer, Dawn re-evaluated her life and ended her affair with Henry, even though he had finally left his wife for her. She was also reunited with her eldest son, Trent, who had run away to be with his father in Scotland. When he returned and gave her the moral support that she needed. Dawn still feared for her daughter Lulu's future, concerned that the breast cancer was hereditary.

ERICA MEETS HER FATHER

After the long quest to track down her natural father, Erica's first meeting with retired Geordie trucker Jackie Brown did not go as she had hoped. When Jackie told her that he had trained himself not to think of her, she fled back to Cardale, avoided his phone calls and refused to speak to him when he later turned up at The Beeches.

However, they did make friends before Jackie returned to Newcastle. He apologised for his previous remark, explaining that not thinking of her was his way of coming to terms with the situation. Erica told him that, even though she had never met her mother, she did miss her. Erica then explained her bizarre behaviour to Andrew, to whom she had given the cold shoulder after her first meeting with Jackie.

Erica finally meets her natural father, Jackie Brown (John Woodvine), after discovering that her mother died in a car crash.

DAVID FIGHTS THE SYSTEM

Sean Hollings, who found it difficult to care for his Down's syndrome brother alone, was detained at Cardale police station after brawling with youths who had teased Jason. Later, Jason was admitted to hospital after suffering an electric shock from welding equipment at Sean's garage.

When hospital tests revealed that he had heart failure and about a year left to live, David asked for him to be placed on a transplant programme, but he was turned down by consultant Dr Martin Byford. Outraged at what he saw as prejudice,

David waged war on the system, calling on Byford at home, talking to the transplant committee, organising a petition and getting the story on the front page of the *Derby Evening Telegraph*. Embarrassed by the adverse publicity, Jason was granted a hearing and recommended for a heart transplant on his own merits. He just had to wait for a suitable donor.

CLARE FACES A DILEMMA

After a spell of helping out at The Beeches, Clare Shearer was offered a job at the Brompton Day Centre, helping patients with psychiatric problems. Before she had time to accept, her plans were thrown into turmoil when she discovered that she was pregnant.

To prevent damage to the foetus, Clare – whose manic depression was being controlled by lithium – had to stop taking her medication. This left Clare and David with the dilemma of continuing with the pregnancy and risking Clare becoming sick again or having an abortion. After taking the job, Clare eventually decided to go ahead with the pregnancy.

TRAVELLING MATT RETURNS

Matt Gibson returned to Cardale after seven years of globetrotting. His parents, Jake and Annie, welcomed him, but were shocked by his frail appearance.

When Matt told Andrew that he thought he had hepatitis B, the GP persuaded him to go to The Beeches for a series of tests. While awaiting the results, Matt tried to recapture time with his parents, Jake and Annie. He went along, with most of Cardale, to a retirement

Anne Gibson (Gwyneth Powell) is delighted when son Matt (Andy Robb) returns but concerned at his frail appearance.

party for his father, who had been the village postman.

When Matt saw his first love, Marie, he taunted her mild-mannered husband Chris, who floored him with a punch after Matt insisted that Marie still loved him. In hospital, a doctor discovered that he had a hereditary condition called Wilson's disease, which had symptoms similar to hepatitis B but also included dementia, and the sufferer often had a history of a rebel streak. Andrew warned Matt that unless he had treatment he would die. Matt returned to his parents and told them that he was home to stay.

• **Andy Robb**, who acted prodigal son Matt Gibson, was subsequently seen as Brian Tilsley's killer, Darren Whateley, in *Coronation Street*. Matt's parents, Annie and Jake, were played by **Gwyneth Powell**, previously in *Emmerdale* and *Grange Hill*, and **Geoffrey Hutchings**, best remembered from *Maigret*.

SHORTHOSE SHORTCHANGES THE BEECHES

The Beeches had no choice but to accept the tide of change that came with the opening of Norman Shorthose's village pharmacy. It meant the closure of the GPs' dispensary, but David advised that, rather than lose out completely, they should follow the example of other practices in the area and start a prescription collection service.

When Norman Shorthose (Clive Swift) opens a pharmacy in Cardale, forcing the closure of The Beeches' dispensary, David finds the chemist more than a pain in the neck.

ANDREW LEAVES FOR LIVERPOOL

Life was looking rosy for Andrew as he settled into his new house – until older sister Chrissy Booth phoned with the news that their mother, Rosaleen, was gravely ill. While Erica moved into his cottage, Andrew travelled home to Liverpool, where he decided to stay and care for his mother after doctors told the family that she was suffering from lung cancer and had only a short time to live.

Erica was given a frosty reception when she eventually went to Liverpool to meet the Attwood family. They thought she was too upmarket for Andrew, and Chrissy claimed that she wasn't a patch on his ex-wife, Kirsty. But Erica remained understanding and reasoned that her visit had not been at a good time. She returned home and was surprised when Andrew arrived shortly afterwards, having rowed with his mother.

• **Deirdre Costello** acted Mrs Heap, whose house Andrew bought. Her previous television roles had included Gina Fletcher in *Coronation Street*, Linda Preston in *I Didn't Know You Cared*, Sue in *Sounding Brass*, Cathy Marlene in *The Nesbitts Are Coming*, Lynn in *Law and Order*, Rachel Wilde in *Crossroads*, Joan in *Big Deal*, Colin's Mum in *London's Burning* and Calley's Mum in *Grange Hill*.

When Andrew returned to Liverpool, his cancer-ridden mother, Rosaleen, was played by **Barbara Ewing**, previously noted for her roles as Dora in *Sam* and Agnes Fairchild in the sitcom *Brass*. **Kate Fitzgerald**, who acted Andrew's sister, Chrissy Booth, was memorable as shopaholic Doreen Corkhill in *Brookside*. She also starred in the West End production of *Shirley Valentine*.

Exterior filming was done on location in Liverpool, but interiors of Rosaleen's small terraced house were set up at Central's Nottingham studios.

CHILD ABUSE NIGHTMARE

When Andrew first went to Liverpool, Erica felt isolated when she became embroiled in a child abuse case. She reported the case of 11-year-old Neil Rushton when he told her that he was being sexually abused by his stepfather, Peter Doyle, a well-liked Cardale resident. As a result, Erica felt the full force of village disapproval. She was refused service in local shops, and her car was sprayed with graffiti.

On the day of the trial, Erica was called to testify in court against Peter and to treat his father, Bob, who suffered a serious stroke in the court waiting room. Bob's condition eventually stabilised in hospital. In court, Peter was found guilty and sentenced to ten years in prison.

• Carol, the wife of convicted child abuser Peter Doyle, was played by **Sally Baxter**, who was cast as Lisa O'Shea in the ill-fated soap *Albion Market* and Maggie Daniels in the detective series *Anna Lee*, alongside Imogen Stubbs. Jennifer Kemp, Peter Doyle's barrister during the child abuse court case, was played by **Zienia Merton**, whose many TV roles include Sandra Benes in the Gerry Anderson live-action sci-fi series *Space 1999*.

MORE TROUBLE FOR ERICA

After a difficult labour with her first child, Jade, Anne Channon was anxious for her next baby's entrance into the world to be as easy as possible. She had chosen to have a home birth, which Erica had promised to attend with community midwife Mary Ravensdale.

However, Erica almost missed the event when The Beeches' receptionist Joanne Pearson – who was jealous that former love Andrew was now dating Erica – had a row with the doctor, walked out on her job and did not pass on the message that Anne was in labour. Erica made it in the nick of time but, when Anne ran into trouble in the third stage, the GP went to pieces and panicked blindly. Fortunately, the midwife kept her cool and guided Erica. After being taken to hospital, Anne underwent a blood transfusion and made a good recovery.

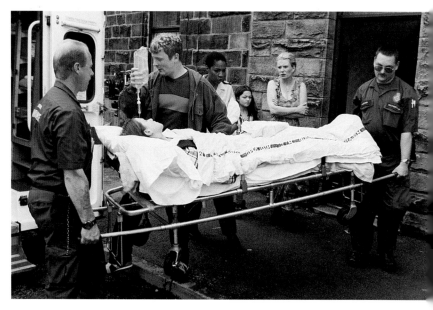

Erica watches in frustration as Anne Channon (Mairead McKinley) is rushed to hospital for a blood transfusion after the home birth of her baby.

BAD TIMES FOR ANDREW

Andrew had been back in Cardale for just a week when he surprised Erica at one of their favourite beauty spots with a romantic marriage proposal. As a token of his love, he offered her the confirmation present that his father had given him. Andrew was cut to the quick when Erica refused him. She felt that the timing was all wrong and that he was still in a highly emotional state about his mother.

Andrew went into a sulk and refused to speak to Erica. He moved into the spare room before the pair eventually made their peace and Andrew returned to Liverpool.

Back home, Andrew finally came close to understanding his mother before she died. As he sat at her bedside, Rosaleen explained that, although she had appeared hard

- **Del Henney,** who acted Andrew's dead father, Frank Attwood, in a dream sequence, appeared in *Coronation Street* in 1971 as footballer Eddie Duncan, who stole Irma Barlow's heart. In recent years, he has appeared in series such as *A Touch of Frost*, *Jonathan Creek* and *The Bill*.
  Yet another former *Street* star, **Maggie Jones**, played Dr Landstone, the GP of Andrew's

sick mother, Rosaleen, in *Peak Practice*. Maggie acted Deirdre Rachid's mother, Blanche Hunt, in *Coronation Street* after playing Sam's grandmother, Polly Barraclough, in the classic Granada Television series *Sam*. Her sitcom roles include David Jason's mother in *Lucky Feller*, Glenda in *Rosie*, bingo-loving widow Mrs Mason in *Lovely Couple*, Mrs Nesbitt in *The Nesbitts Are Coming*, Ivy in *Sharon and Elsie* and Nan in *South of the Border*.

• Alice North's initially unwilling companion on a pensioners' outing to Kedleston Hall was arthritis sufferer Alby James, played by **Geoffrey Bayldon**, who enthralled young viewers in the title role of *Catweazle* and as the Crowman in *Worzel Gummidge*.

He is used to being ill on television, following roles as patients in *Casualty* and *Where the Heart Is*. The more arduous task in *Peak Practice was* taking to a rowing boat with Margery Mason, as Alice, and becoming stranded in the middle of a river after losing an oar. The scene was filmed one afternoon and through the night.

'We were lucky because it wasn't a cold night,' recalls Geoffrey. 'The main task was to make it look real in that I could just about navigate the boat and that pain caused me to lose the paddle. It was easier than we expected, particularly because there were two stunt people hidden in the water guiding the boat. I loved that episode as much as anything I've done for a long time. I liked the character and it had something to say about the man's fear of going into a home.'

Also on the pensioners' outing, but well away from the water, was actress **Irene Sutcliffe** as Maisie. She is best known as shopkeeper Maggie Clegg in *Coronation Street* during the sixties and seventies, and Gloria in more recent sitcom *The 10%ers*.

on Andrew's father, she had loved him.

Her battle with lung cancer was a bitter one and, despite an increase in painkilling drugs, her agony grew worse. She could take it no longer and asked Andrew to help her to die. Even though he had support from Dr Landstone, his mother's GP, he found her request a difficult one to come to terms with. However, Andrew finally acceded to her wishes and, with his sister Chrissy, administered a lethal dose of morphine and Rosaleen slipped away peacefully.

PENSIONERS' UNLIKELY ALLIANCE

When Alice North found herself on an OAP trip to Kedleston Hall with 70-year-old Alby James, the pair formed an unlikely alliance. They had not spoken for 40 years, since Alby – a devout socialist – had fallen out with Alice's husband, Bob, during a strike.

Arthritis sufferer Alby James (Geoffrey Bayldon) loses an oar as he takes Alice North on an unscheduled rowing-boat trip.

Bored by the old folks' singsong, Alice and Alby stole the bus and set off for an adventure to a nearby beauty spot renowned for its healing waters. Alby, who suffered from severe arthritis, and diabetic Alice made their way down to the water's edge where they sat down and talked of how Alice's daughter Patricia wanted her to live with her in Canada and the likelihood that Alby would have to go to live at Whiteacres Retirement Home.

Rather than attempt to walk, Alby decided to make their way back down the river in a rowing boat. But the pair became stranded when Alby lost the oars. As darkness descended, David – who had organised the outing – arrived, plunged into the water and pulled them to safety. Alby accepted that he could no longer cope in his own house and, with David's help, moved into the home.

PRIEST'S MYSTERY ILLNESS

When Vicky Johnson suffered from stomach pains and diarrhoea, Andrew suspected that her Crohn's disease – a chronic inflammation of the gastrointestinal tract – had flared up again. But Catholic priest Father Matthew Corlon warned the GP that her symptoms might have more to do with Vicky's distress at the first anniversary of her sister's death.

Andrew treated the priest's words with disdain and rudely told him that he did not have to listen to him. However, Father Corlon turned out to be right when Vicky – unable to deal with her feelings of loss – took an overdose of antidepressants. Father Corlon raised the alarm after discovering a suicide note that Vicky had posted through his front door. Vicky was saved just in time

and the incident brought her grieving family closer together.

Father Corlon, meanwhile, was not a well man. He consulted Andrew, who discovered that he was suffering from thrombocytopenia, a problem with his blood-clotting mechanism. The priest was admitted to hospital for further tests and Andrew warned him that leukaemia was a possibile cause.

As the priest counselled Andrew over his feelings for his mother, the GP began to warm to him. Andrew was amazed that Father Corlon's test results showed there was no definable cause for his condition.

> • Father Matthew Corlon, who was admitted to hospital with a blood problem, was played by Irish actor **Jim Norton**, who appeared in the films *Adolf Hitler: My Part in His Downfall* and *Hidden Agenda*, as well as playing Albert Einstein in *Star Trek: The Next Generation* and three different roles in the sci-fi series *Babylon 5*. **Alison Skilbeck**, who acted Matthew's consultant in hospital, previously played Flora Dunn in *Head Over Heels* and Dr Sarah Eastwood in *Soldier Soldier*.

DR NICK FINALLY GETS NICKED

Dr Nick Goodson joined The Beeches as a locum while Andrew was away in Liverpool. He seemed eager to make friends with his new colleagues, telling them the tragic story that he was a widower who had cared for his dying wife. He also offered to help David in running the practice's fund.

But Nick was a conman who put money before patients. Unbeknown to his colleagues, he was charging for sick notes and nearly caused the death of Sean Welch, who suffered from a perforated ulcer, by waiting to see him until after 10pm, when he was paid more money for a callout.

Nick then began to involve patients in secret drugs trials and ensnared chemist Norman Shorthose in a prescription fraud. He also set about wooing practice manager Kim Beardsmore, from whom he hoped to obtain £3,000 of The Beeches' money with his sweet talk, dinner and red roses. One of the dodgy doctor's patients nearly died from septicaemia when Nick used unsterile instruments to remove a cyst under local anaesthetic.

Nick kept up the pretence until the bitter end as his crimes were uncovered one by one and his supposedly dead wife arrived at The Beeches with their children. David stepped in to prevent Nick's escape with a powerful punch to the jaw and his wife walked out of The Beeches and Nick's life.

• Mr Jordan, a pensioner who cut his head open after demonstrating cartwheels to his granddaughter and was caught up in crooked Dr Nick Goodson's prescriptions scam, was played by **Keith Marsh**. The actor was seen as four different characters in *Coronation Street* between 1961 and 1980, but is best known for his sitcom roles as gardener Ralph in *George and the Dragon*, Wendy Craig's father in *And Mother Makes Three*, Jacko Jackson in *Love Thy Neighbour* and Henry in *The Gaffer*. He also played Thomas Clough in *Crossroads* in 1985.

Erica has doubts about the tragic tale told by locum Nick Goodson (Thomas Lockyer) when he arrives at The Beeches.

CLARE BREAKS DOWN

One legacy of Nick Goodson's time at The Beeches was the seeds of doubt he had sown in David's mind as to the state of Clare's mental wellbeing. She began to deteriorate under David's anxious scrutiny, becoming obsessed about cleanliness and hygiene to the point that she scrubbed the house from top to bottom and insisted that the family ate only natural, organic food.

James 'Mac' Macarty (Paul Bown) puts a spanner in the works when girlfriend Anna Bradshaw (Caroline Langrishe) crosses paths with ex-boyfriend David.

A chance meeting with David's first love, Anna Bradshaw – who ran a landscape business with her alcoholic boyfriend, Mac, and his son, Cal – finally triggered off Clare's manic depression again. David offered Mac help in drying out as he showed signs of cirrhosis of the liver, but Mac could not seem to kick the bottle.

Clare became obsessed with Anna and constantly questioned David about her. He was finding his wife's behaviour impossible to deal with and seemed to be taking refuge in Anna and Mac's problems, calling on them nearly every day.

Mac was later admitted to hospital, where he had a finger amputated after his poor circulation prevented an infected cut finger from healing. This time David managed to persuade Mac to give detox another try.

Clare's state of mind grew worse. She was convinced that she was carrying Anna's baby, believing that they were in some way connected. She refused to take mild antidepressants and demanded that David hand over Mac's care to Andrew. David refused and considered having Clare sectioned.

When enlarged veins in Mac's throat ruptured, he nearly died. Fortunately, he recovered and Clare, in a calmer frame of mind, talked to David about their future together.

But the couple had a problem of a different kind when David discovered they were £5,000 overdrawn at the bank, had a string of unpaid bills and their house developed subsidence. David was furious when the insurance company denied liability. He was even more down in the mouth when Clare announced that they would sort out their money problems by cutting down on food and going without any holidays for a year.

• **Paul Bown** played alcoholic James 'Mac' Macarty but is still best remembered for his role as Malcolm in the long-running sitcom *Watching*.

   Caroline Langrishe became the first of three stars to play two different parts in *Peak Practice*. Five years after playing Dr Susan Lees in the first series, she returned as Mac's girlfriend, Anna Bradshaw. In between, she was seen as auctioneer Charlotte Cavendish in two series of *Lovejoy* and Lady Anne Camoynes in *Sharpe's Regiment* and *Sharpe's Justice*.

ERICA'S ASBESTOSIS CRUSADE

Erica put her heart and soul into helping Charlie Fields and his ex-workmates find out what had caused their chest complaints. The men had all been employed by Howetts car plant, installing brake linings, 15 years earlier. Two of the men, Sam Melchett and Patrick Connor, had since died and now X-rays revealed that Charlie had scarring to his lungs.

Erica was convinced that the men had all suffered from asbestosis – an inflammation of the lungs caused by inhaling asbestos particles. With the help of Liam Bannerman, Patrick's best friend, she was able to connect the men's deaths with their work at the factory through a classified health and safety report that confirmed that the workers were at high risk from the deadly, incurable disease. Armed with this information, Erica encouraged Charlie and the families of the dead men to seek compensation through the courts.

STARING DOWN A BARREL

Schizophrenic Tricia Fletcher arrived in Cardale to stay with her brother, Steve, and his wife, Alison, who was unaware of her illness. Tricia wanted to come off her medication because she was concerned about the tablets' side effects. She ignored Andrew's advice to reduce the dosage under supervision and tipped the drugs away.

Tricia's condition worsened and Clare Shearer, working at the Brompton Day Centre, seemed to be the only person to whom she could talk. Hearing voices inside

Tricia Fletcher, a diagnosed schizophrenic, causes anxiety in Cardale as she holds Andrew and Clare hostage inside The Beeches.

• **David Hargreaves** became the second star to play a second role in *Peak Practice* when he acted Charlie Fields, who had been exposed to asbestos at work. Since appearing four years earlier as the Rev. Neil Winters, his other television parts had included Sir Anthony in *BUGS* and Dad in the sitcom *Bloomin' Marvellous*. Charlie Fields' wife, Val, was played by **Anny Tobin**, who acted mother Mary Ellen O'Brien in the television adaptation of Catherine Cookson's *The Fifteen Streets*.

Bernard Gallagher, who acted Charlie Fields's friend Arthur Bannerman in *Peak Practice*, is a veteran character actor who in recent years played Jo Weston's father, Graham, in *Heartbeat*. One of his two sons, John Bannerman, was played by **Bob Mason**, the third actor to play two roles in *Peak Practice*. He had previously appeared as Roger Wyatt in 1995.

Asbestosis victim Patrick Connor was acted by **Breffni McKenna**, who played Dave Gould in the latter days of *Crossroads* and Donald Forbes in director Ken Russell's television version of *Lady Chatterley*. Mary Melchett, widow of another asbestosis victim, Sam, was played by **Zena Walker**, who in the seventies had played Victoria in *Albert and Victoria* and Susan Lampton in *Man at the Top,* and has more recently guest-starred in Agatha Christie's *Poirot* and *Heartbeat*.

her head, Tricia began to lose her hold on reality and was terrified of Andrew, whom she believed to be 'The Controller' who had killed her (very much alive) three-year-old nephew, Ben.

Steve locked Tricia in a room for her own safety when a duty psychiatrist considered Tricia to be a danger to herself and others. With no hospital beds available, Tricia remained there until one could be found. Alison left, taking Ben with her. Tricia's psychotic behaviour then came to a head when she escaped and held Andrew and Clare at gunpoint at The Beeches.

As armed police surrounded the building, Andrew was shot in the shoulder as he tried to wrestle the shotgun to the ground. Tricia then tried to shoot herself in the head, but the gun was empty. She ran out of The Beeches and the police, believing that she was still a threat, opened fire, shooting her once in the shoulder. Andrew's cries that her gun was empty went unheard and he dashed over to help her as she lay critically wounded on the ground. Tricia was rushed to hospital, where doctors gave her a good chance of survival.

• **Eve Steele** took the role of schizophrenic Tricia Fletcher, who held Andrew Attwood and Clare Shearer at gunpoint in The Beeches. Eve previously played *Coronation Street*'s Anne Malone, who became obsessed with Curly Watts. She returned to the *Street* in 1998 as his boss.

Tricia's brother, Steve Fletcher, was played by **Richard Hawley**, best known as Helen Mirren's sidekick, Det. Insp. Richard Haskons, in *Prime Suspect* and Chris Lennox in two series of *The Vet*. The police inspector who took charge when the surgery came under siege was acted by **Peter Cleall**, forever to be remembered as troublesome Eric Duffy in the school sitcom *Please Sir!*

LAURA LEAVES FOR ALBANIA

Practice nurse Laura Elliott decided it was time to bid farewell to The Beeches after successfully applying for work with Voluntary Service Overseas in Albania. Everyone was sorry to see her go, including Norman Shorthose, who bombarded her with chocolates, flowers and a gold St Christopher. He told Laura that he loved her, although she reminded him that she could not return his feelings.

SURROGATE LOVE TRIANGLE

When pregnant Lizzie Tate had an abortion after developing kidney failure, she thought she had lost her chance of ever having a baby. But her sister, Helen, agreed to act as a surrogate mother, against Erica's advice. The issue became complicated when Helen revealed that she was in love with Lizzie's husband, Ian, although they had never slept together.

Ian was so involved with Helen and her pregnancy that he had less time for his sick wife. On the day that Ian and Helen admitted their feelings for one another, Lizzie blacked out and fell down the stairs at their home. Later discovered by Erica, she was rushed to hospital. On recovering, she told Ian that she wanted to leave the area after the baby's birth and make a fresh start.

Helen, on discovering Lizzie's plans, called at her sister's home where she exploded with the pent-up anger she felt at being the one who had stayed at home to care for her parents while Lizzie had led a life of her own. Lizzie in turn was devastated to hear of the attraction that existed between her sister and Ian. After a heart-to-heart with her husband, Lizzie agreed to give their marriage another chance.

SUPERMARKET PROTEST VICTORY

Ian and Lizzie Tate found themselves on opposite sides when proposals for a Cardale supermarket were put forward. Lizzie worked for the local authority and backed the plans, but Ian supported residents who felt that the development would sound the death knell for village shops.

Protesters, led by Norman Shorthose, left the property developers in no doubt about their feelings when they barricaded the entrance to the proposed site. The villagers cheered and claimed victory as the developers conceded defeat and beat a hasty retreat.

> • Another seventies star to resurface in *Peak Practice* was **Ian Lavender** as Mr Neville, whose plans to develop a supermarket on the edge of Cardale were opposed by locals. The actor is still often seen in repeats of the classic sitcom *Dad's Army*, in which he played Private Pike.
>
> One of the opponents of the supermarket plan, Ian Tate, who nearly had a fling with his sister-in-law who was having a surrogate baby for him and his wife, was played by **James Gaddas**, previously seen as Dr Robert Nevin in the hospital drama *Medics*, Det. Insp. Latham alongside Joanna Lumley in the comedy-drama *Class Act*, Jim Reaper in *Backup* and David Cash in *Family Affairs*. Earlier, he had appeared in *Coronation Street* as Robert Prescott, yuppie brother of Dawn Prescott, who conned her boyfriend, Mike Baldwin, out of £150,000 in a Spanish property deal.

DOCTORS HIT A BRICK WALL

When ex-RAF serviceman Rob McBride turned up at The Beeches with a mystery illness, Andrew began to suspect Gulf War syndrome and encouraged Rob to go on the Ministry of Defence's Medical Assessment Programme. His suspicions were compounded when he discovered that Rob's young daughter, Jessie, had a heart murmur: there was speculation that congenital problems were linked to contact with radioactive materials by one or both parents, as Rob and other Gulf War veterans had experienced.

As David and Andrew investigated the condition, they discovered that the servicemen had been injected with vaccinations covered by the Official Secrets Act and could get no explanation. Rob blamed himself for Jessie's heart problem. Unable to take any more, he tried to kill himself but was saved just in time. He agreed to go on the assessment programme and decided to fight the MoD to get answers.

ERICA POPS THE QUESTION

Andrew was over the moon when, at a Volvo owners' rally in Ashbourne, Erica took the initiative and asked him to marry her. He accepted her proposal with a kiss and arrived at The Beeches the next day with a crate of champagne to toast his happy announcement. Erica, wrapped up in her asbestosis case, failed to turn up, so Andrew cracked open the champagne and told everyone of their engagement in her absence.

BABY BORN ON HEN NIGHT

Erica spent her hen night round the roulette wheel at a Nottingham casino with her friends from Cardale. After an evening of drinking, she was unable to come to the rescue when Clare went into labour prematurely. The expectant mother was bundled into the back of Billy Matters's taxi and when the baby could wait no longer, Kim Beardsmore and Billy delivered it, while Erica slept in the front seat. Billy was honoured when David and Clare named the baby boy William.

Andrew has reason to celebrate after Clare survives without her anti-depressants to give birth to son William.

WEDDING DOUBTS SOWN

In the days leading up to her wedding, Erica had to deal with an outbreak of Legionnaires' Disease at Whiteacres Retirement Home after it claimed the life of elderly resident Nora Oaks. When health inspectors closed down the home to deal with the contamination, which they had traced to the old showers, Erica helped to find temporary homes for the residents. Meanwhile, the owners of Whiteacres, Kate and Peter Lewis, faced financial ruin

because they did not have insurance cover to pay for the work being carried out.

One inmate, Bob Hampton, went to stay with his daughter, Jane, while his wife, Martha, was ill in hospital. Erica chanced upon him in the village church, where she was to be married. Bob was praying for Martha, but he broke off to talk to the troubled GP. He told Erica of his love for Martha and their wedding in the village church. Unwittingly, he made Erica face up to her doubts when he said, 'If you didn't feel the same, you wouldn't be able to marry your young man tomorrow.'

JILTED AT THE ALTAR

Erica had spent the week before her wedding at The Manor Hotel. Potential disasters came thick and fast. Andrew's suit was not ready until the last moment, the band that he had booked for the reception turned out to be a country and western group, and the caterers pulled out at short notice. But Andrew and best man David breathed a sigh of relief when Chloë and James agreed to deal with the food. With their daughter, Sarah-Jane, as Erica's bridesmaid, the wedding was turning into a real family affair.

On the wedding day, Andrew arrived at the church late when his car refused to start and he had to run to collect his suit. As he headed for the church in his top hat and tails, he was stopped to help Norman Shorthose, who had collapsed with angina in his shop.

Back at The Manor Hotel, Erica revealed her doubts to barmaid Dawn Rudge, who tried in vain to talk her round. Erica arrived at the church in her everyday clothes to tell Andrew that she could not marry him. She simply did not feel as much for him as she should. Andrew was brokenhearted and begged Erica in vain not to abandon the wedding. Erica walked away, leaving Andrew to tell the guests that the wedding was off. Later, Erica told David that she was taking two weeks' holiday and was not sure whether she would be back.

Erica's dream about her wedding to Andrew (below) turns into a nightmare for him when she arrives at church to explain that she cannot go through with it (right).

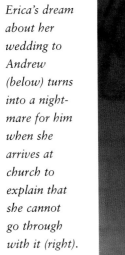

• Kate Lewis, owner of Whiteacres Retirement Home, was played by **Noreen Kershaw**, the first actress to play Shirley Valentine in Willy Russell's acclaimed one-woman stage play when it opened in Liverpool. On television, Noreen had previously acted Lynne Harrison in *Albion Market*, Jimmy Corkhill's long-suffering girlfriend Kathy Roach in *Brookside* and Brenda's mother, Mrs Wilson, in *Watching*. As a director, she has also worked on the Granada Television serials *Coronation Street* and *Springhill*.

Andrew C Wadsworth, a musical star of West End shows such as *Godspell*, *Troubador*, *Songbook*, *Sweeney Todd*, *Oklahoma!*, *Blood Brothers* and *Guys and Dolls*, played Kate's son, Peter Lewis.

INDEX